More Moto Collectibles

Leila Dunbar

4880 Lower Valley Rd. Atglen, PA 19310 USA

Published by Schiffer Publishing Ltd.
4880 Lower Valley Road
Atglen, PA 19310
Phone: (610) 593-1777; Fax: (610) 593-2002
E-mail: schifferbk@aol.com
Please write for a free catalog.
This book may be purchased from the publisher.
Please include $3.95 for shipping.
Try your bookstore first.

We are interested in hearing from authors
with book ideas on related subjects.

Contents

Acknowledgments

Thanks to Howard for being the gambler and Martha for holding the bank together when the occasional boxcars came up. Thanks to Dave Gaylin for his contribution of photos, values, and information for Chapter 8, "Motorcy-cling in Film." Thanks to Bob "Sprocket" Eckardt, Barry and Arline MacNeil, John Sawazkhi, and auction consign-ors for contributions from their collections; Thanks to David Wasserman and Martin Jack Rosenblum for their time; thanks to Tom Funk and Eric Killorin at *Mobilia* magazine for letting me be their "biker chick writer." Thanks to Cris Sommer Simmons and Pat Simmons for their continued enthusiasm and support. And, finally, thanks to all the great people from around the world, riders and non-riders, who have participated either by consigning and/or bidding in our "Moonlight Kid" motorcycle memorabilia auctions, keeping the history and image not only alive, but thriving.

—Leila Dunbar

Introduction

So, you want to start collecting motorcycle stuff? Well, you've come to the right place.

Maybe you are a dyed-in-the-denim biker who has been riding since you were knee-high to a Scout throttle. Maybe you just recently loosened your tie, discovering the joys of the open road after being closed up in that computer-lit cubicle far too long. Or maybe you've seen women like Wynonna (no last name required) perched on her Fat Boy (oh, what an image) and decided you too wanted to feel seven hundred pounds of steel between your legs.

Regardless, you're now joined at the grips with an estimated five million United States motorcycle enthusiasts in a quest for speed and serenity. This second volume of *Motorcycle Collectibles*, like the first book, is designed to guide you in your search for mementos from your two-wheeled adventures. Let's face it, almost everyone collects something, whether it's old signs, toys, cars, or Slim Whitman records (why, I don't know—it's an imponderable). From our earliest days, we humans have shown the need to gather, horde, and trade.

Congratulations—you have entered a world where leathers are worn like chic armor, a man named Willie G. is king, many of the horses ridden are branded Harley, and an empty route lined by trees and lakes is truly the road to Camelot.

There are two basic types of motorcycle collectibles—the first category covers historic items that were produced originally as accessories, sales materials, giveaways, etc. A few of the many items falling into this category would be original dealer catalogs, jewelry, posters, signs, and clocks.

The second category includes limited edition or market-made collectibles such as cycle models and plates, banks, reproduction signs, and toys. These were produced to be instant collectibles, without any other purpose. The concept is that these items will be assimilated into collections and over time demand will rise and exceed supply, causing values to also rise (like posthumous Elvis plates, etc.).

The ride so far has been a great hill climb for both categories. Thanks to the increased exposure of these collectibles in both mainstream and collector magazines and the internet, to documentaries about motorcycling, to reference books on the market, motorcycle collectibles have made

the Kneivel leap from trash to treasure. Two major auction houses deal with collectors from Aberdeen to Yokahama, trying to fill bidders' requests for everything from chainbreakers to racing jerseys.

Items that bring the most interest and continually appreciate tend to be three-dimensional and/or pre-1930 vintage. Pre-1920 Indian sales catalogs, by far more colorful and dynamic than their Harley-Davidson counterparts, will sell for $100-$500, depending on condition, i.e., if they have greasy oil smudges or torn pages, don't expect to pay top dollar. At the high end, a Indian dealership sign from the 1940s will have collectors running to their piggy banks or mortgage lenders to get the $1,000-$3000 that it will take to pry it (gently, of course) off the wall of the current owner.

Notice the wide ranges in price. Like any market, stock or otherwise, collectibles live through cycles and fluctuations. Condition, rarity and current desirability mean everything in valuation. *There is no such thing as a set in stone price guide, Virginia.* Reference books can be helpful in determining relative values, but that's it. The real determination of the current market is out there at the swap meets, antique shows and auctions. So, make sure you go forth, ask questions and finger the goodies. Books educate, but they don't buy and sell—people do.

Therefore, if you are a beginner collector, note that there are risks inherent in collecting. Like motorcycling, it's not for the faint of heart and shouldn't be jumped into whole "Hawg" by the inexperienced. To build a solid collection and to ensure a pleasant experience, you must take the time to learn about the collectibles market and what you want to collect. You need to meet and develop relationships with other collectors and dealers. And, above all, make sure you buy things that you like—you are the person who's going to live with it. What's the point of a good deal when you don't like the piece?

And, finally, buy the best condition that you can afford. The biggest mistake that beginning collectors make is that they buy pieces in poor condition because they're cheaper, instead of spending the extra money for the same items in excellent condition. They're afraid to spend too much. Just the opposite tenet is true: The items bought in great condition are the ones that will hold their value over time. If you do your homework, it won't take you long to figure out when you should stretch and spend for that rare piece in great condition.

Until you become comfortable in your collecting skills, the good news is that there are many historic collectibles that are still affordable and tasty for beginners and/or those with Happy Meal pocketbooks. A 1930s copy of the *Harley-Davidson Enthusiast* magazine, first printed in 1916 and the longest continually published motorcycle magazine in the country, will only set a collector back $10 to $30. These magazines are packed with information about the times and the sport of motorcycling.

Indian postcards, pens, matchbooks, issues of the *Wigwam*, later brochures, and small tools are still reasonably priced in the $10 to $50 range. Likewise, some of the American Motorcyclist Association Gypsy Tour awards, which commemorate annual biker gatherings sponsored by the AMA, are also still affordable, particularly the later pieces, dating from the 1950s. A small group of collectors

shoot for the whole set of awards, 73 years worth, a much more costly and time-consuming hunt, but they do look very attractive displayed on the mantel—much more politically correct than a mounted Bullwinkle head.

Where will the market go in 1997 and beyond? Should you buy? Sell? Go watch *The Great Escape* again? From what we have seen over the past ten years, prices have risen appreciably and steadily and the motorcycle collectibles market still hasn't hit its peak. As more and more newcomers find happiness on their Hawgs (the AMA reported more than 40,000 new members in 1996, bringing membership to 211,000) and the public perception of bikers moves from convict to cool, new collectors have joined the old-timers in celebrating the ninety-five-plus year history of the motorcycle.

So gas up and gather your goggles and gauntlets, we'll be taking a long trek through collectible corridor—no helmets required!

Straight from the Hawg's Mouth
Advertising, Signs, and Oil Cans

What's that line, the more things change, the more they stay the same?

I guess that could be said about the logic behind advertising—expose potential buyers to an experience they won't forget and make sure your logo is linked with that experience.

Before the days of websites, telemarketing, and (gasp) even television and radio, companies had to rely on the power of print advertising, either in newspapers and magazines, and the allure of the showroom. Point-of-sale promotions in the form of handouts, literature, and product identification were very important. Imagine taking a trip into a showroom—behind a shiny new Harley are a series of hot posters, babes, hunks, and movie stars on bikes, with print below that you completely ignore, illustrating this year's exciting improvements. "Now is a better time than ever to buy a Harley, . . ." You go to check the time and staring down at you is a light-up bar and shield clock. The salesman hands you a bunch of color brochures, decals, and a gold-plated eagle pin just for coming in and saying howdy.

Now, back that up seventy years, change the bike models and babes and hunks to skirted and suited young ladies and gentlemen on those bikes and sidecars, and you get the idea. If a potential customer made the trek into town to contemplate a purchase, the dealership was not going to let him get away—and that's still the case today.

Dealerships such as Harley and Indian heavily decorated their showrooms with big litho color posters; tin and porcelain signs with their distinctive logos; neon and light-up clocks, all promoting the thrill of riding their cycles, the new models for that year, and the (always) many new improvements, both aesthetic and mechanical, to the current crop of bikes. If Indian was promoting its new 1916 Powerplus Motor or 1920 Scout model, or Harley was announcing a new line of deco paint options in 1933, or Excelsior was boasting about the Super X model, it was all done through bold advertising.

This Authorized Dealer enamel-on-steel, flanged sign, circa 1940s, is one of the most desirable Indian signs because of its color and size. As Indian shrunk production and models while reorganizing after World War II, these signs were seen less and less often. 26 1/2" x 24 1/2". ($500-3,000) *Courtesy of the Dunbar Moonlight Kid Collection.*

This set of four-color Indian photo slides from 1916 was originally shown in a Wisconsin movie house to promote E. A. Franzen, a Delavan dealer. Found in the original mailing carton from Manhattan Slide & Film Co, NYC, they each measure 4" x 3 1/4". Eighty years later and still in great shape, they could still be dropped into the projector between newsreels. *Courtesy of Dunbar Moonlight Kid Auctions.*

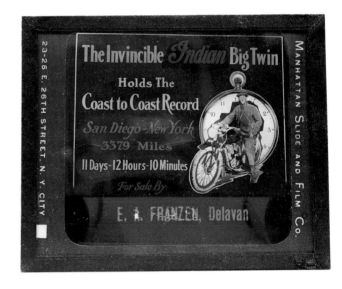

A movie house slide shows the 1916 Indian Sales Catalog. The first year of the power-plus motor, Indian was the motorcycling market and racing leader in the early days. Indian's catalogs offered bright color and dynamic graphics, as opposed to Harley's muted, silent grey fellow. ($250-500, set of four slides.) *Courtesy of Dunbar Moonlight Kid Auctions.*

Movie house slide shows the 1916 invincible Indian Big Twin, holder of the coast-to-coast record—3,379 Miles in eleven days, twelve hours, and ten minutes. The record-setting rider, Erwin "Cannonball" Baker, captured the romance of motorcycling, racing many makes of cycles and making his mark by breaking many transcontinental endurance records between 1910 and 1930. 4" x 3". ($250-500, set of four slides.) *Courtesy of Dunbar Moonlight Kid Auctions.*

Movie House Slide Shows 1916 Indian Cradle Spring Frame Big Twin Power Plus Motor. only $275, the Power Plus Motor was Charles B. Franklin's contribution to Indian after original engineer and partner Oscar Hedstrom retired in 1913. 4" x 3". ($250-500, set of four slides.) *Courtesy of Dunbar Moonlight Kid Auctions.*

Another 1916 Movie House Slide: "Don't Motor Alone—Take Her Along in an Indian Sidecar" and "Double the Pleasure of Your Outing." Hey, the offer of freedom, romance, and a day off the farm was really nice, but why did women always have to sit in the sidecar? 4" x 3". ($250-500, set of four slides.) *Courtesy of Dunbar Moonlight Kid Auctions*

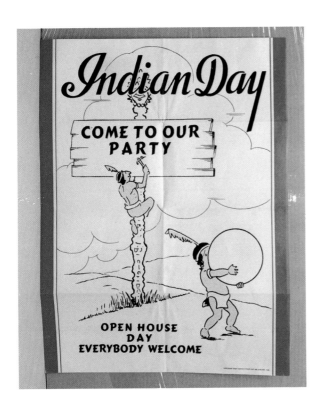

Indian announced its 1940 annual George Washington's birthday open house with this poster featuring an Indian climbing a totem pole, nailing up an invitation. 21" x 28". ($100-300) *Courtesy of John Sawazkhi.*

A nice summer fishing scene with sidecar is pictured on this 1917 Firestone Tire calendar, part of a four-piece set with one picture for each season. ($100-400) *Courtesy of the Dunbar Moonlight Kid Collection.*

Why Indian chose to promote their new 1940 models in this cartoon-fashion poster—instead of using big, bold photos showing the new flared fender skirts—is anyone's guess. A nice poster, but certainly not the one a Chief, Sport Scout, or 4 owner would really want hanging above his bike. Artist Ed Goodman, 20" x 30". ($100-300) *Courtesy of Dunbar Moonlight Kid Auctions.*

After two years of producing the "upside down four," Indian returned to a standard intake over exhaust engine for its 1938 "4." This poster is an announcement of "38 New Features." 28" x 41" ($150-400) *Courtesy of John Sawazkhi.*

This Harley-Davidson neon dealership clock, circa late–1940s, is highly desirable. 18" x 18". ($1,000-3,000) *Courtesy of the Dunbar Moonlight Kid Collection.*

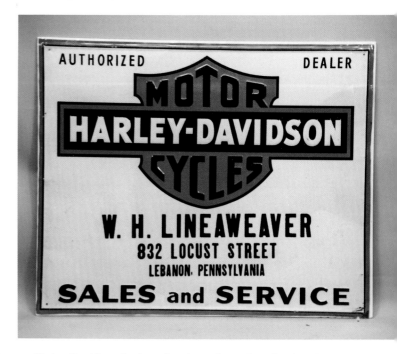

Columbia Motor Goggles Display, circa 1930s, features a uniformed policeman on his trusty bike looking sharp and feeling safe. The eight pairs of sunglasses are bent in the center in a design engineered to break the wind. ($100-400) *Courtesy of Bob "Sprocket" Eckardt.*

Harley-Davidson tin sign advertises sales and service for a Lebanon, Pennsylvania, dealer. Circa 1940s, 29 1/2" x 23 1/2". ($500-1,200) *Courtesy of the Dunbar Moonlight Kid Collection.*

This Harley-Davidson decal on glass could be ordered by dealers and was used for shop or window displays. Goodstix, Circa 1950s, 19" x 6". ($50-250) *Courtesy of Bob "Sprocket" Eckardt.*

Harley "50" Poster touts "180 miles to the gallon" in an attempt to capture a light-weight motorcycle market that has been opting for Japanese models Printed on flame-retardent matting, 55" x 48". ($100-400) *Courtesy of Bob "Sprocket" Eckardt.*

Harley-Davidson light-up display with clock has a center panel for advertisements. Circa 1960s, 4' x 10" x 4' Deep. ($300-800) *Courtesy of the Dunbar Moonlight Kid Collection.*

Motorcycle companies have always had to fight for market share. In the early 1900s, hundreds of manufacturers burst onto the market—Yale, Pope, Thor, Flying Merkel, Reading-Standard, to name just a very few, who chased the Big Three (Indian, Harley-Davidson, and Excelsior) down the road and whose dreams ended before they could get around the curve. Signs and materials from this age, particularly from companies that only lasted a few years, are very rare. Likewise, there is a smaller market for these pieces, as the makers are less known than the Big Three. While the market may be narrower, the competition between the collectors will still be keen because of the dearth of these pieces.

After World War I, with the advent of a cheaper automobile and a shrinking pool of potential customers, the Big Three pushed motorcycling as a sport and as economical, dependable transportation. All three companies stayed in business by exporting cycles and selling to police departments.

Also, they all realized the importance of selling ancillary items to their customers in order to keep them coming back between major purchases. After all, if you bought an Indian, wouldn't you want authentic Indian oil in your tank? Who would know better than the company that made the motorcycle what grade of oil would make the cycle run its best? It didn't matter that other companies subcontracted the oil to the makers, the cans held their logos.

The items shown here, as in Volume I, are just a smattering of the signs, posters, clocks, etc. that could be out there to find, lying in the back of closed dealerships or tucked away in quiet collections. Many were simply destroyed, given to scrap drives or discarded without sentiment when the dealership went out of business. Others have simply disintegrated with time, although restoration can bring back their beauty and a bit of youth.

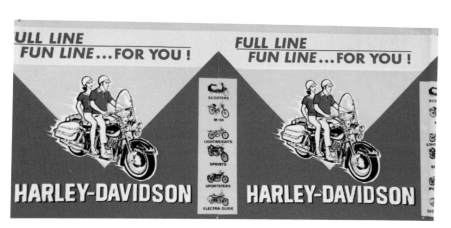

Harley continues a longtime tradition of promoting couple togetherness with this 1965 poster that introduces an electric starter, marking the first year for Electra Glide and the last year for Pan Head 106" x 48". ($200-700) *Courtesy of Bob "Sprocket" Eckardt.*

Founded in 1939 in Lincoln, Nebraska, Cushman manufactured scooters and small industrial trucks. Enamel-on-steel flange sign, 20" x 14". ($200-500) *Courtesy of the Dunbar Moonlight Kid Collection.*

At its low point in 1984, with stock at $3 a share, it seemed no one was insisting on anything. Tin sign, circa 1980s, 17" x 23 1/2". ($50-300) *Courtesy of the Dunbar Moonlight Kid Collection.*

This tin Kool cigarettes sign featuring a Harley is a collectible of the future. ($10-50) 17" x 35", *Courtesy of the Dunbar Moonlight Kid Collection.*

Three inserts for this Harley-Davidson Poster feature 1940 champions Jack Pine winner Ted Konecny, Daytona winner Arthur "Babe" Tancrede, and speedway Champion Lou Guanella. Circa 1940, inserts, 21" x 30". ($200-700) *Courtesy of the Dunbar Moonlight Kid Collection.*

Chances are, if you walked into a Harley dealership in the 1950s, you'd see this oil parts manual stand at the parts counter. ($50-200) *Courtesy of Dunbar Moonlight Kid Auctions.*

Harley-Davidson shed light on its product with a lamp and shade that doubled as advertising. The company discovered that merchandizing acessories and ancillary products could bring extra profits. Circa 1940s, nickel-plated lower ring and upper cap, 35" tall with shade. ($200-500) *Courtesy of the Dunbar Moonlight Kid Collection.*

Harley-Davidson AMF empty cardboard case for premium grade motorcycle oil. Circa 1970s. ($25-75) *Courtesy of the Dunbar Moonlight Kid Collection.*

Oilzum sponsored a number of automotive and motorcycle racers from the earliest days. Oilzum Motorcycle Oil decal, Circa 1950s, 4" x 4". ($10-50) *Courtesy of the Dunbar Moonlight Kid Collection.*

A note—as with any collectible, condition, vintage, rarity, and graphics are the four qualities that contribute to value. And the market is unpredictable. The set of 1916 Indian slides, in mint condition, from a movie house in Wisconsin, only sold for $350 in a recent auction, much less than what I would have priced them at as a dealer. Yet the Indian Authorized Dealer sign, in very nice condition, sold for $5,500. Are the slides only worth $350 and the sign really worth as much as $5,500?

The answer is yes and no to both. Both are worth those prices because that's what someone was willing to pay for them at one particular auction. However, if a dealer put the sign at that price, he'd probably wouldn't sell it for a long time. Competition, or lack thereof, also affects values. The slides, early and rare, should really be worth quite a bit more, probably in the $500-$1,000 range for the set, even though I put them in the book for $250-$500, but they were overlooked in the sale and someone got a very good buy. The point is that it's very hard to pin down any market—auctions have items that sell high and sell low—only those who enjoy collecting and are willing to accept risk should get into the game. After all, the excitement is in the hunt and the learning process.

Generations of Harley-Davidson Motorcycle Oil are represented in these quart containers. The earliest is the orange and black Genuine Oil, 1930–50s ($50-200). Pre-luxe in the upper left corner dates to the 1950s ($50-200) and the Pre-luxe in the two lower rows are from the 1960s ($25-75 each). The AMF Preluxe cans are late '60 s–early 1970s ($10-50 each). Sno-Oil was only made for a short period of time during Harley's fling with RV's ($40-100). Premium II and Power Blend are post AMF ($10-40 each)and, yes, Harley is #1 ($10-30 each). *Courtesy of the Dunbar Moonlight Kid Collection.*

A pair of Harley AMF spray paint cans and one Two-Cycle Lubricant can, circa 1970s. ($10-20 each)

A trio of Indian quart oil cans, circa 1930s–40s. ($50-200 each) *Courtesy of the Dunbar Moonlight Kid Collection.*

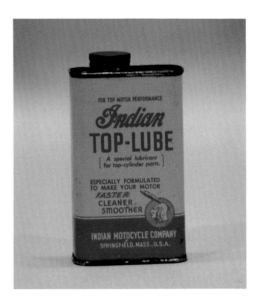

Can of Indian of Top-Lube engine lubricant, circa 1930s. ($50-150) *Courtesy of the Dunbar Moonlight Kid Collection.*

Indian Chain Oil can, circa 1930s, with paper label, 5 1/2" tall. ($20-50) *Courtesy of the Dunbar Moonlight Kid Collection.*

A trio of quart oil cans from the Wigwam, 1930s–1940s, are all popular with collectors. ($50-150 each) *Courtesy of the Dunbar Moonlight Kid Collection.*

The one-quart Oilzum HP Motorcycle Racing Oil container from the 1960s featured six motorccycles on top. (Scarce, $50-150) *Courtesy of the Dunbar Moonlight Kid Collection.*

Quarts of Coop 4-Cycle Motorcycle Oil, Kendall GT-1 Special, and Amalie 4-Cycle Motorcycle Oil from the 1960s–70s. ($10-20 each) *Courtesy of the Dunbar Moonlight Kid Collection.*

Group of Castrol Motorcycle Oil Cans from 1960s–80s. ($5-30 each) *Courtesy of the Dunbar Moonlight Kid Collection.*

Castrol Super 4-Stroke Motorcycle Oil, one-quart container. (. $10-30) *Courtesy of the Dunbar Moonlight Kid Collection*

Nitrol 9 fuel additive for motorcycles, 4-ounce can. ($5-20) *Courtesy of the Dunbar Moonlight Kid Collection.*

Gunk Motorcycle Carb Cleaner, 12-ounce can. ($5-20) *Courtesy of the Dunbar Moonlight Kid Collection.*

Chapter 2

Read All About It
Books and Magazines

Like most motorcycle memorabilia, the most interesting and sought-after books and magazines come from the earliest days of the sport. This is simply because, in the early 1900s there were so many makes of motorcycles from which to choose. By the time World War I began, there were but a saddlebag's worth of brands left to fight over a shrinking customer base.

Before the days of the *Love Boat* and the Travel Channel, books were the vehicle that transported our adventurous souls to all parts of the world. Children's book series like *The Motorcycle Chums*, *Tom Swift*, *Bert Wilson*, *Tom Slade*, and *The Motorcycle Five* gave little boys (and girls, too) vicarious two-wheeled thrills in between chores. For adults, how-to-repair motorcycle books were (and are) popular.

As the motorcycling craze came hot on the heels of the bicycle craze at the turn of the twentieth century, the first motorcycling publication actually adapted itself. In 1902, to capture the rapidly growing new audience, *The Bicycle World* became *The Bicycle World and Motorcycle Review*.

Later on, *Bicycle Illustrated* would become *Motorcycle and Bicycle Illustrated*.

Interest in motorcycling started in the East, with a majority of the manufacturers in New England and New York, but rapidly moved west and southwest where riders could enjoy their motorcycles year-round. To serve newcomers to the sport, in 1910 *The Western Motorcyclist and Bicyclist* was founded in Los Angeles, followed two years later by the *Pacific Motorcyclist*.

Two other trade publications, *Motorcycling* (which even became a weekly for a time between 1910-1914) and *Motorcycle Illustrated* covered the efforts of the newly formed national organization, the Federation of American Motorcyclists and kept up to date on the endurance and board track races that were stirring imaginations all over the country. There was also news of the motorcycle clubs that were popping up like pistons all over the country. And, as the motorcycle rider was usually his own best mechanic, these magazines were libraries of know-how, from coaxing a start to tweaking cranky motors and on-the-road repairs.

The March and April 1916 editions of *The Harley-Davidson Dealer* magazine, Volume 5 No.s 3 & 4, include articles about parts, trends, suggestions, offers, news, specifications for dealers, and a long article in April about Harley's involvement with Pursuit of Pancho Villa. There are great showroom and factory photos, too. These magazines are much rarer than the earliest and scarcest *Enthusiast* magazines. ($50-200 each) *Courtesy of Dunbar Moonlight Kid Auctions.*

Issues of Harley-Davidson's *The Enthusiast* from 1917–1918. The *Enthusiast* was first published in 1916 and has become the longest, continuous motorcycle publication, still being produced today. *The Enthusiast* has always promoted motorcycles for touring, camping, fishing, and as a conduit to other outdoor sports. ($50-200 each) *Courtesy of Dunbar Moonlight Kid Auctions.*

Postwar *Enthusiast* issues focused on Harley racing wins, motorcycle club news, touring, the promotion of new models, and, of course, accessories. These *Enthusiast* issues are dated August–December 1952. ($5-20 each) *Courtesy of the Dunbar Moonlight Kid Collection.*

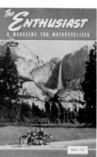

A complete leather-bound copy of all twelve issues of *The Enthusiast* for 1944. Issues during the war years focused on Harley's efforts for Uncle Sam as well as featuring various movie and music stars on their Harleys, doing their part for victory. ($100-400) *Courtesy of Dunbar Moonlight Kid Auctions.*

The Enthusiast magazines, January–April 1953. ($5-20 each) *Courtesy of the Dunbar Moonlight Kid Collection.*

The Enthusiast, May–August 1953 ($5-20 each.) *Courtesy of the Dunbar Moonlight Kid Collection.*

The Enthusiast, September-December 1953. ($5-20 each) *Courtesy of the Dunbar Moonlight Kid Collection.*

The Enthusiast, January, February, April, and May 1954. ($5-20 each) *Courtesy of the Dunbar Moonlight Kid Collection.*

The Enthusiast, June-September 1954. ($5-20 each) *Courtesy of the Dunbar Moonlight Kid Collection.*

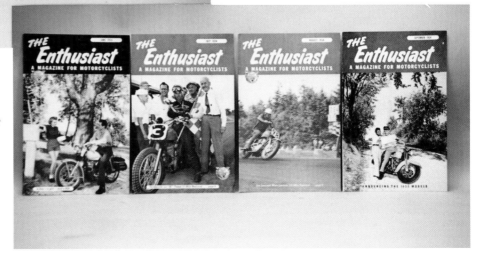

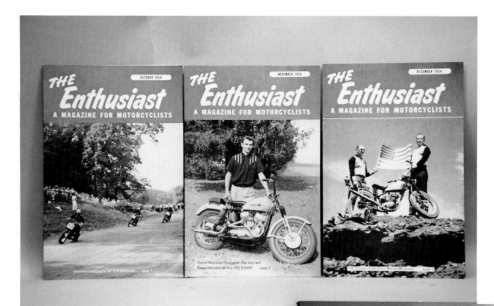

The Enthusiast, October–December 1954. ($5-20 each) *Courtesy of the Dunbar Moonlight Kid Collection.*

The Enthusiast, May-August 1955 ($5-20 each) *Courtesy of the Dunbar Moonlight Kid Collection.*

The Enthusiast, January–April 1955. ($5-20 each) *Courtesy of the Dunbar Moonlight Kid Collection.*

The Enthusiast, September–December 1955. ($5-20 each) *Courtesy of the Dunbar Moonlight Kid Collection.*

Early motorcycle magazines are great historical pieces, with ads from the many makers that enjoyed brief success but have long since retired to the scrap heap. For example, there was Thor, the creation of Aurora Manufacturing of Illinois, which produced motors for Indian for several years and offered its own model. It had moderate success on the racing circuit, but with the onset of World War I, the company returned to its more lucrative appliance business. Orient, of Waltham, Massachusetts, is hailed as the first American motorcycle, beginning production in 1899 and beating out Indian by two years. But Orient only lasted until 1910. Excelsior, one of the Big Three, was the motorized sector of the Schwinn bicycle empire. It produced both Excelsior and later Henderson four-cylinder motorcycles until Ignatz Schwinn abruptly called it quits in 1931. Flying Merkel, which made a brief splash on the racing scene with a surprisingly powerful engine, sold 10,000 units, then retreated back to bicycles. Pope and Columbia, both of Hartford, Connecticut, and both offshoots of their parent bicycle and automobile companies, were brief contenders. And Iver Johnson, of Massachusetts, the only known black maker, also produced firearms and bicycles.

Many, many more obscure brands, such as Reading-Standard, Schickel, MM (Marsh-Metz), Emblem, American Eagle, Yale, Dayton, Black Hawk, Haverford, etc. are found chuffing on these magazine pages. All fell victim to a number of problems, including an automotive industry that cut prices, increased wages, and the shortage of materials brought on by World War I.

These and the two-hundred-plus other makes that could afford the advertising were on the pages of these early magazines, promising less vibration, smooth-running motors, complete reliability, speed, comfort, economical transportation, adventure, and freedom.

Likewise, many ancillary companies advertised in these magazines. Goodyear, Goodrich and Firestone all ran large ads for their tires. Electrical lamp makers like Sol competed in print, and there were plenty of manufacturers ready to supply clothing, leggings, and goggles to fight off oil spatters. Other accessories to be seen on the pages included sidecars, clip-on motors to turn a bicycle into a motorcycle; mirrors, horns, and sirens to alert horses, pedestrians, and horseless carriages, spark plugs, magnetos, locks, special seats and tandem setups, and anything else that could be of use on a motorcycle.

The Enthusiast, January–April 1956. ($5-20 each) *Courtesy of the Dunbar Moonlight Kid Collection.*

The famous Elvis issue of *The Enthusiast*, May 1956. Harley has always enjoyed the glory of star-ownership, from Clark Gable and Elvis to Sly Stallone and members of ZZ Top. ($50-300) *Courtesy of the Dunbar Moonlight Kid Collection.*

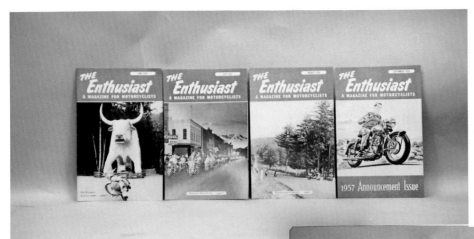

The Enthusiast, June–September 1956. ($5-20 each) *Courtesy of the Dunbar Moonlight Kid Collection.*

The Enthusiast, January–April 1957. ($5-20 each) *Courtesy of the Dunbar Moonlight Kid Collection.*

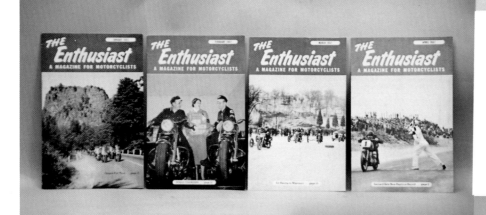

The Enthusiast, October–December 1956 ($5-20 each) *Courtesy of the Dunbar Moonlight Kid Collection.*

The Enthusiast, May, July, and August 1957. ($5-20 each) *Courtesy of the Dunbar Moonlight Kid Collection.*

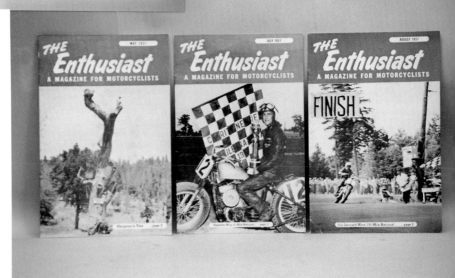

A smiling Indian overlooks a group of people enjoying winter motoring on the Christmas Issue cover of the *Indian News*, Volume I, No. 1, December 1925. The back cover features childrens' bikes, a scooter, and a coaster in use. ($50-300) *Courtesy of the Dunbar Moonlight Kid Collection.*

Indian Motocycle News magazines, 1941–1945, include race results, club news, photos & snapshots, Vaughn Monroe visiting the Indian factory and riding a bike, biker servicemen news with photos, biker servicemen news and photos, 8" x 10" and 8" x 11". ($10-40 each) *Courtesy of Bob "Sprocket" Eckardt.*

Alan Ladd graces the cover of the July–August issue the *The Indian Magazine*. The Spring 1949 issue features Cary Grant, Robert Ryan, Lizabeth Scott, racing and travel photo articles, an article authored by Robert Stack, new Indian models, Bob Feller and Vaughn Monroe photographed on Bikes, and more. 8 1/2" x 11 1/2". ($10-40 each) *Courtesy of Bob "Sprocket" Eckardt.*

Like other special interest *Motorcycling Magazine* February 22, 1912, offered new horizons, new adventures, and speed (in racing). On the cover, a lost cyclist gets directions from a friendly farmer. Ads include Indian, Waverly, Wagner, Pierce, Flying Merkel, Yale, Schickel, Thor, and New Era. Almost all (except Indian) would stop making motorcycles by 1920, casualties of a wartime economy and Henry Ford's use of assembly line technology which lowered the cost of making automobiles, savings which he passed onto the consumer. ($30-60 each) *Courtesy of the Dunbar Moonlight Kid Collection.*

Motorcycle Illustrated magazine, January 22, 1914, and November 27, 1913. This was one of several motorcycle magazines that chronicled exploits during the heyday of motorcycling. Established in 1906, the publication flourished in the heady days of motor-dromes and multiple makers, petering out in 1932 after changing its name to *The New American Motorcyclist And Bicyclist*. Just before World War I, the bi-weekly publication featured ads from all the big makers of the day—Yale, Dayton, Reading-Standard, Excelsior, Henderson, Emblem, Flying Merkel, Pope, and, of course, Indian, the leader, and Harley, the brand that was just picking up steam. ($30-75 each.) *Courtesy of the Dunbar Moonlight Kid Collection.*

The cover of *Motorcycling Magazine* dated November 14, 1912, features a photo from Wisconsin, Ads include Goodyear, Yale, Excelsior, Flying Merkel, Flanders, Eclipse, Reading-Standard, Pope, H-D, Eagle, Silent Indian, plus articles about the Federation of American Motorcyclists, race reports, new Excelsior Models. 64 Pages. ($30-60) *Courtesy of the Dunbar Moonlight Kid Collection.*

In 1914, Indian was the world's largest selling motorcycle in the world, with 25,000 units sold and more than $700,000 in profits.

Motorcycling puts "The Winter Rider" on the cover for January 2, 1913. Inside ads include rare makes like Jefferson, AMC, Michaelson, Monarch and Deluxe. Indian dominates with a back-page ad. 60 pages. ($30-60 each) *Courtesy of the Dunbar Moonlight Kid Collection.*

A Brush at Hawthorne Track, Chicago, in 1913

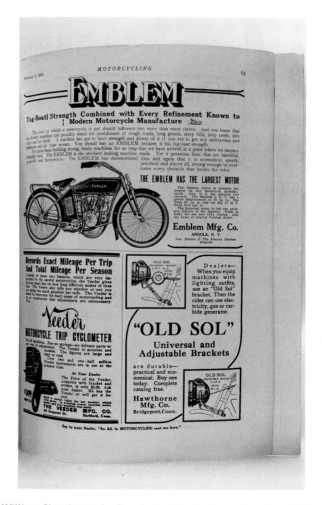

Motorcycling magazine put dirt track racers on the cover for its February 2, 1914, issue, with news about Hawthorne Track in Chicago, in 1913. There were many photo articles and news about travel, racing, and mechanical tips. Ads include Excelsior Autocycle, Thor, Henderson, Flying Merkel, Dayton, Pirate, Limited, Emblem, Reading-Standard, Indian, and Iver Johnson & Yale Bicycles. 64 pages. ($30-60 each) *Courtesy of the Dunbar Moonlight Kid Collection.*

William Shrack was the force behind the Emblem Mfg. Co, which made both single and twin cycles from 1909-1925. After WWI, Emblem only made a lightweight V-twin for export.

These early magazines are priceless views into the motorcycling culture of the early 1900s, truly the industry's halcyon days. Because of the wealth of information they have about early and short-lived makes, these magazines are coveted by many collectors. Prices range from $10 to $100, depending on the condition, year, and cover (racing covers are more valuable than Sunday touring covers, for example.)

Harley-Davidson did not stand out in the early magazines, but would mark its own territory permanently in 1916 with the inception of its owners' magazine, *The Enthusiast*. Like the early magazines, *The Enthusiast* featured touring, racing, and club news, all from a Harley standpoint, which is quite understandable. Eighty-six years later, *The Enthusiast* is still printed four times a year, making it the longest continually running motorcycle magazine. As I have noted a number of times, copies of *The Enthusiast* are still a very good buy on the collectibles market because many copies still exist. In Volume I, the earliest examples of *The Enthusiast* are shown. In this volume, the run is continued into the 1950s. Pre 1920 copies are still coveted, 1920s copies sought after, 1930s-40s magazines are popular and reasonable, 1950s and newer copies should be very inexpensive.

On the other hand, copies of Harley's rival publication, *Indian News*, are harder to find and more expensive to acquire. Like their sales catalogs, the covers of *Indian News*, particularly those of the 1920s, are far more dynamic and colorful than *The Enthusiast*, which were in black and white, usually with some type of bucolic biking scene. This was okay, but, hey, the era was called the "Roaring Twenties," not the "Snoring Twenties" and Indians did roar, at least on paper. Because of their relative scarcity and graphics, 1920s–30s copies of the Indian News usually sell for double *The Enthusiasts*. Once you get to the 1940s–50s, though, the magazine (like the model line) falters and the value drops to about equal with the Harley publications. Indian's final 1950s try, *Pow Wow*, sells for $5-25 a copy, as the roar was snuffed out by decades of bad decision making and, finally, inferior quality control and engineering.

The cover art for *Motorcycling* magazine's March 9, 1914, issue was a solo rider near Erie, Michigan. 56 pages. ($30-60)
Courtesy of the Dunbar Moonlight Kid Collection.

Yale Motorcycles were made by Consolidated Manufacturing Company out of Toledo, Ohio, from 1902–1915. One of the motorcycle pioneers, Yale made both single- and twin-cylinder cycles, leaving the market too soon in 1915.

"No More Solitary Pleasure" announces the March 16, 1914,issue of Motorcycling, picturing a family of four in sidecar rig. 64 pages. ($30-60) *Courtesy of the Dunbar Moonlight Kid Collection.*

"If it passes you, it's a Flying Merkel" was a phrase one might have overheard in 1910 racing circles. Like many of the early companies, Merkel enjoyed a brief sprint on the motorcycling scene. Engineer Joe Merkel developed a new spring frame and compact spring fork. The improvements were seen in 1910 when Merkel rider Fred Whittler defeated Indian star Jake DeRosier. Merkel continued to be a force in board-track racing until 1914. The company introduced a spring-powered self-starter that year, and it proved a disastrous decision. Undercapitalized and feeling the effects of a wartime economy, Merkel was forced to close down in 1915.

A woman picks flowers next to sidecar bike on the cover of *Motorcycling,* June 29, 1914. With a a theme of getting away from it all; the magazine had an article on the Dodge City Races, picnic trips, and ads for Harley, Pope, Excelsior, Klaxon, Thor, Yale, Flying Merkel, Henderson, Emblem, Limited, Dayton, and, on the back cover, Indian. 64 pages. ($30-60) *Courtesy of the Dunbar Moonlight Kid Collection.*

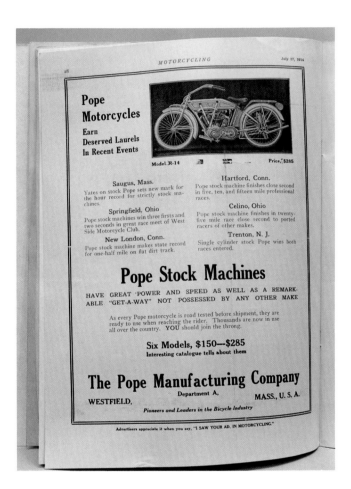

Thor, made by the Aurora Automatic Machinery Company of Chicago, got its start in 1903 as subcontractor for Indian pocket valve engines. The company developed a line of single- and twin-cylinder cycles which, contrary to this ad, did not fare well in competition against Indian and Excelsior. The company chose to concentrate on its more lucrative home appliance business in 1915.

Pope never quite found its place in motorcycling. Begun as a clip-on spinoff from Hartford, Connecticut's booming bicycle business, Pope achieved some success with an overhead valve engine in 1910. The only other maker besides Indian at the time to have an overhead-valve motor in 1913, Pope won a flurry of second-tier races, but the company was in disarray following the death of its founder and the line was discontinued in 1915.

"Rambling in California" is featured on the cover of *Motorcycling*, July 27, 1914. Ads include H-D, Pope, Excelsior, Yale, Flying Merkel, Henderson, Emblem, Limited, Dayton, Champion, Bosch, Indian. 64 pages. ($30-60) *Courtesy of the Dunbar Moonlight Kid Collection.*

Carl Goudy, Winner of 100-Mile at Rockford

Carl Goudy on his Excelsior, winner of the 100-Mile Race at Rockford, is featured on the cover of the August 17, 1914, *Motorcycling*. Articles include "The Effect of War on the Cycle Trade." Excelsior, in business since 1907, is now ranked Indian's chief competitor. In 1912, Lee Humiston, on an X, became the first sanctioned motorcylist in the world to be officially timed at 100 miles per hour. Carl Goudy was a perennial Excelsior rider in the 1910s. Ads include H-D, Pope, Excelsior, Yale, Flying Merkel, Henderson, Emblem, Limited, Dayton, Champion, Bosch, Indian. 64 pages. ($30-60) *Courtesy of the Dunbar Moonlight Kid Collection.*

Motorcycling took readers to Skyline Drive, Colorado, on the cover of the January 18, 1915, issue. There were articles about "Best Race Performances" and "Cycling as Better Than Booze." Ads included H-D, Excelsior, Smith Motor Wheel, Miami, Emblem, and Indian. 64 pages. ($30-60) *Courtesy of the Dunbar Moonlight Kid Collection.*

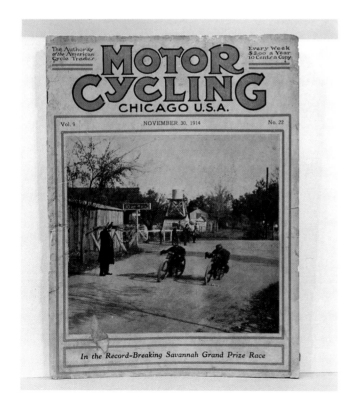

In the Record-Breaking Savannah Grand Prize Race

The Savannah Grand Prize Race was featured in the November 30, 1914, issue of *Motorcycling* magazine, with race results and articles. Ads include H-D, Pope, Excelsior, Smith Motor Wheel, Reading-Standard, Henderson, Emblem, Dayton, and Indian. 64 pages. ($30-60) *Courtesy of the Dunbar Moonlight Kid Collection.*

The Miami Motorcycle Company took over Flying Merkel in 1910, with nearly 10,000 units sold yearly from 1910–1915. The company also produced an ultra-light pedal cycle, sold alongside its bicycle.

Motorcycle Illustrated magazine August 19, 1915, featured a "Motorcycliste" on a Dayton along with ads by Firestone, Excelsior, Flying Merkel, Pope, Emblem, Reading STD, Thor, and Federation of American Motorcyclists. 9" x 12", 60 pages. ($30-60) *Courtesy of Bob "Sprocket" Eckardt.*

Motor Wheels were popular add-ons for bicycles, providing extra power without a lot of extra weight.

Motorcycle Illustrated magazine, July 13, 1916. The back cover advertised Davis Sewing Machine Co. Motorcycles. Inside ads included Champion, Cygnet, Flying Merkel, Cleveland, Excelsior, Goodyear, Harley-Davidson, Pope, Henderson, Indian, Reading STD, Rogers, Thor, Pullman, and Federation of American Motorcyclists. 9" x 12", 56 pages. ($30-60) *Courtesy of Bob "Sprocket" Eckardt.*

The 1951 *Motorcycling Digest* presented the official program for the 1951 New England Gypsy Tour & 100-Mile National Championship Road Race and a list of the entrants. 8" x 12", 40 pages. ($25-75) *Courtesy of the Dunbar Moonlight Kid Collection.*

The April 7, 1951, issue of the *Saturday Evening Post* featured a painting of children admiring "Tex's" Harley. The finished product on the magazine cover was sort of a cross between Norman Rockwell and Fonzie. ($50-150) *Courtesy of the Dunbar Moonlight Kid Collection.*

Motorcycling & Bicycling magazine, April 30, 1919, had a cover ad for Rollfast Bicycles and a back cover ad for Cleveland Motorcycles. Even though eighty-five percent of domestic production had been shut down by the war, some companies were still hanging in there. Inside this issue, more than thirty-five manufacturers and trade names were represented,. 9" x 12", 112 pages. ($30-60) *Courtesy of Bob "Sprocket" Eckardt.*

This poster is of the artist Stevan Dohanos' double-signed proof of original art work for the 1951 *Saturday Evening Post* cover. The three boys are admiring a bike owned by "Tex" Keeler of Georgetown, Connecticut. 25" x 34". ($300-1,200) *Courtesy of the Dunbar Moonlight Kid Collection.*

In 1933, *The Pacific Motorcyclist* became simply *The Motorcyclist* as the magazine became the official publication of the American Motorcyclist Association, which is still printed monthly for the 200,000-plus AMA members. Early copies of *The Motorcyclist* are more valuable than later copies, as less were printed and less have survived.

Later copies of motorcycle magazines, from the 1960s, have not hit their stride yet, but probably will in the next few years.

Four 1955 issues of *American Motorcycling*—January, May, August, and October, including Indian, BSA, Jawa, Triumph, and Harley ads; lots of racing articles; American Motorcyclist Association, and Motor Maids. ($5-25 each) *Courtesy of the Dunbar Moonlight Kid Collection.*

American Motorcycling magazine went global in April 1952, with ads from domestic makers like Indian Brave, BSA, and Harley, along with information about motorcycling in Japan, Laconia, Etc. ($5-25) *Courtesy of the Dunbar Moonlight Kid Collection.*

The new Harley K line proved a big winner when Paul Goldsmith won the Daytona 200 with the fastest time yet of 94.45 miles per hour, pictured here on the cover of *American Motorcycling*, April 1953. ($5-25) *Courtesy of the Dunbar Moonlight Kid Collection.*

American Motorcycling magazine had a special issue in October 1953 celebrating the fiftieth anniversary of Harley-Davidson. The issue includes a preview of 1954 50th Anniversary Models. ($10-40) *Courtesy of Dunbar Moonlight Kid Auctions.*

American Motorcycling magazine, September 1953, featured the Pirate Treasure Run on the cover; full-page ads from Indian, BSA, and Buco; a Harley 50th Anniversary centerfold; racing and American Motorcyclist Assocation news, and Motor Maid articles. ($5-25) *Courtesy of the Dunbar Moonlight Kid Collection.*

American Motorcycling magazine, March 1954, featured Winter Tour on its cover. Inside were Hall of Fame, Motor Maids, BSA, Indian, and Harley ads. ($5-25) *Courtesy of the Dunbar Moonlight Kid Collection.*

Accessories make the outfit for men and women. Notice that 1954 was still pre-helmet, though the tradition of leather was well established.

Books

Early motorcycle books were of two types. The first were basic how-to guides because the first generation of motorcyclists needed to be their own mechanics since breakdowns happened regularly in out-of-the-way places. The second type took readers to the race tracks, the war, and other faraway, exotic locales where only two wheels, a motor, and an imagination could go.

Bert Wilson's Twin Cylinder Racer, hardcover, JW Duffield. ($20-60) *Courtesy of the Dunbar Moonlight Kid Collection.*

ABC of the Motorcycle, copyright 1916, by W.J. Jackman, a master engineer of the early motorized era. The book has 222 pages divided into 22 chapters beginning with Daimler's first motorcycle and progressing through each mechanical part from carburetor to ignition. The book also covers road troubles, cost, tires, and dont's, and it includes many illustrations. A great read for anyone interested in the origins and early sport of motorcycling. ($30-100) *Courtesy of the Dunbar Moonlight Kid Collection.*

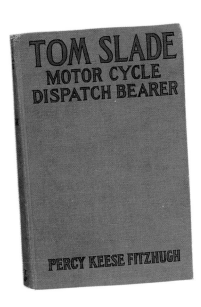

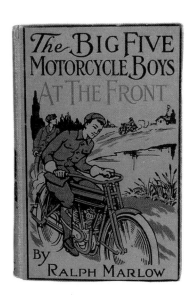

The Big Five Motorcycle Boys at the Front, hardcover, Ralph Marlow. ($20-60) *Courtesy of the Dunbar Moonlight Kid Collection.*

Tom Slade Motor Cycle Dispatch Bearer, hardcover, Percy Keese Fitzhugh. ($20-60) *Courtesy of the Dunbar Moonlight Kid Collection.*

Chapter 3

Dealing in Dreams

Promotional Items

Dealership and club promotional items have always been a way of wearing your allegiance proudly. Motorcycle dealers passed out pins and fobs so brand-loyal customers could carrying them around.

Many pieces were handed out to celebrate a new style or model, like the Indian Saddle Tank Pin, given in 1940 to promote new saddle tank styling, or the Harley V Pin, given out to promote the V-Twin line. You could always pick up a variety of giveaways during sales or special new-model days, such as Indian's traditional Indian Days.

Then, there are special one-year pieces, like the desirable fiftieth anniversary Harley-Davidson tank emblem, which can sell for $200-$500. The great thing about these items is that they're small, so they're easy to display. And the pins can be worn, showing awareness of motorcycle heritage and history.

Note: Beware of reproduction and new giveaway items that can be passed off as vintage. Chapter 10 presents "fantasy items" of this recent vintage. Always ask before you buy.

A smaller but still superbly detailed Harley-Davidson printers block. Bronze, circa 1936, 2" x 1". ($75-150) *Courtesy of Dunbar Moonlight Kid Auctions.*

The Harley-Davidson company sent a package to dealers to create their own promotional materials, including these printers blocks. Bronze, circa 1936, 5 3/4" x 3" x 1". ($100-400) *Courtesy of Dunbar Moonlight Kid Auctions.*

Harley-Davidson printers block. Bronze, circa 1936, 5" x 1 1/8". ($100-300) *Courtesy of Dunbar Moonlight Kid Auctions.*

Harley-Davidson's Victory Logo dominates this 50th Anniversary emblem from 1954. Gold, 2 1/2" x 3". ($100-600) *Courtesy of Dunbar Moonlight Kid Auctions.*

Indian Motocycles folding knife with embossed Indian. Nickel plated with logo, circa 1930s. ($50-200) *Courtesy of Dunbar Moonlight Kid Auctions.*

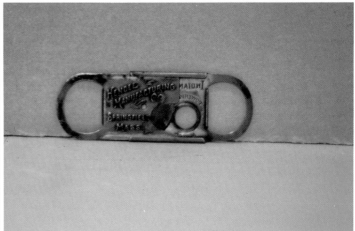

Front and rear views show an Indian Motocycle cigar cutter that advertised the Power Plus Motor. Copper plated, circa 1916, 2 1/2" x 1". (Rare—100-350) *Courtesy of the Dunbar Moonlight Kid Collection.*

Crazy Indian Motocycles pin. Embossed Indian on both sides, circa 1920s. 1 1/2" height. ($50-150) *Courtesy of Dunbar Moonlight Kid Auctions.*

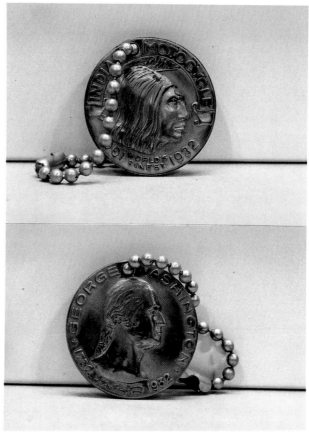

Indian Motocycle's 1932 George Washington's birthday coin, 1901–1932, double sided with classic Indian on reverse side. Used as a pendant or key fob. 1 1/4" diameter. ($50-150) *Courtesy of Dunbar Moonlight Kid Auctions.*

Winged Indian Motocycles pin with full headdress, circa 1930s. ($50-150) *Courtesy of Dunbar Moonlight Kid Auctions.*

Heavily embossed, sterling silver, winged Indian pin, circa 1920s. 2 3/4" long. (Scarce, $200-350) *Courtesy of Dunbar Moonlight Kid Auctions.*

Indian cloth jacket patch, circa 1940s, 4" x 5". ($50-100) *Courtesy of Bob "Sprocket" Eckardt.*

A solemn Indian is pictured on this cloth jacket patch. 7" x 2 1/2". ($50-150) *Courtesy of Dunbar Moonlight Kid Auctions.*

Indian jacket patch with embroidered Indian head. Circa 1940, 7" x 3". ($50-100) *Courtesy of Dunbar Moonlight Kid Auctions.*

Indian saddle tank pin. Circa 1940, 1" long. (Scarce—100-200) *Courtesy of Dunbar Moonlight Kid Auctions.*

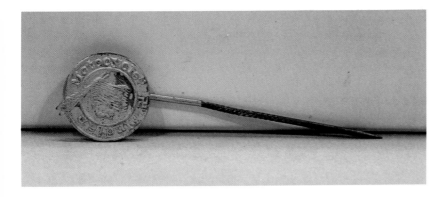

Indian gold embossed metal stickpin. Circa 1940s, 1/2" diameter. ($50-125) *Courtesy of Dunbar Moonlight Kid Auctions.*

This celluloid pinback is a great early button plugging Indian Motocycle-Hendee Manufacturing Co. Circa 1910, 1". ($100-250) *Courtesy of Dunbar Moonlight Kid Auctions.*

Front and rear shots of an Indian dealer giveaway match book. J.C. Hoel, who started the annual Sturgis Motorcycle Rally in South Dakota, is named on the back cover. Circa 1940s. ($25-75) *Courtesy of Dunbar Moonlight Kid Auctions.*

1940s Indian tie clip, silver and blue. ($50-125) *Courtesy of Dunbar Moonlight Kid Auctions.*

Four Indian pins and ribbons recall the Second Annual Indian Rally, July 14-15, 1973; the sixth rally in 1977; the fifth rally in1976, and the 1970 Old Timers Reunion pin and ribbon. ($10-20 each) *Courtesy of Bob "Sprocket" Eckardt.*

A child's party hat was one of many Indian giveaways. Circa 1930s. ($25-100) *Courtesy of Dunbar Moonlight Kid Auctions.*

Motorcycle pendant, 10K gold and mother of pearl. Circa 1930s–40s. ($50-150) *Courtesy of Dunbar Moonlight Kid Auctions.*

Harley-Davidson motorcycle string tie, green cord with brass ends, 1 3/4". ($50-150) *Courtesy of Dunbar Moonlight Kid Auctions.*

Harley-Davidson watch fob with unusual, maker's mark on reverse side. Bronze with leather strap, circa 1930s, 1 3/4" x 1 3/8". ($100-300) *Courtesy of Dunbar Moonlight Kid Auctions.*

1940s Harley-Davidson V twin pin with clasp and shield logo in center. ($100-250) *Courtesy of Bob "Sprocket" Eckardt.*

Harley-Davidson dealer decal. 3" x 2".($10-30) *Courtesy of Dunbar Moonlight Kid Auctions.*

A scarce Harley-Davidson gold-plated, eagle logo pin. 2" x 2". ($100-200) *Courtesy of Dunbar Moonlight Kid Auctions.*

A gold, 1950s Harley tie clip.($75-150) *Courtesy of Dunbar Moonlight Kid Auctions.*

1956 Harley-Davidson belt buckle portrays a group riding through the countryside with the company logo in the top, right corner. 3" x 2". ($75-200) *Courtesy of Dunbar Moonlight Kid Auctions.*

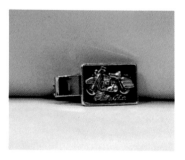

A silver, 1960s Harley Electra Glide tie clip. ($50-125) *Courtesy of Dunbar Moonlight Kid Auctions.*

Harley-Davidson Flathead Twin Engine
Pin. Circa 1930s, 1" x 1". ($50-150)
Harley-Davidson shield logo pin, 1" x 1".
($50-100) *Courtesy of Dunbar Moonlight
Kid Auctions.*

Harley-Davidson belt buckle. Copyright 1984, three-dimensional
accessories like this are the collectibles to watch for in the future.
Manufactured in Chicago, 3 1/4" x 2" x 1/4". ($5-25) *Courtesy of
Dunbar Moonlight Kid Auctions.*

Harley-Davidson pocket watch with a second hand for timing. Circa
1920s, but beware of reproductions. ($300-800) *Courtesy of Dunbar
Moonlight Kid Auctions.*

Solid brass Harley-Davidson belt buckle with enameled oval insert.
Because it was made in Taiwan in 1983, this buckle will probably
not be as desirable as the one from Chicago. 1/2" x 2 1/4". ($5-15)
Courtesy of Dunbar Moonlight Kid Auctions.

Harley-Davidson screwdriver "Compliments of Boyer Cycle, Easton,
PA." Nickel plated, 5". ($25-75) *Courtesy of Dunbar Moonlight Kid
Auctions.*

Solid brass Harley-Davidson belt buckle with enameled oval insert. Because it was made in Taiwan in 1983, this buckle will probably not be as desirable as the one from Chicago. 1/2" x 2 1/4". ($5-15) *Courtesy of Dunbar Moonlight Kid Auctions.*

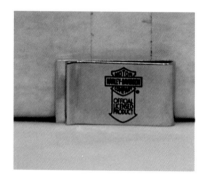

Harley-Davidson money clip touts "Genuine Parts & Accessories" on the front, and on the rear proves that it is with—"Official Licensed Product." Circa 1984, 2" x 1". ($5-20)

Match holder in shape of Harley-Davidson Preluxe can with original matches. Circa late-1950s–'60s, 2 3/4". ($25-100) *Courtesy of Dunbar Moonlight Kid Auctions.*

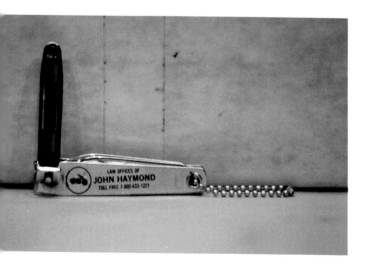

American Motorcyclist Association belt buckle with a club logo in rop right corner, Harley in the lower corner, and "Doris" in raised letters. Nickel plated with cloisonne, circa 1950s, manufactured by Hookfast, Providence, Rhode Island, 2 3/4" x 1 7/8" ($5-40—maybe more if your name is Doris) *Courtesy of Dunbar Moonlight Kid Auctions.*

A scarce Harley-Davidson gold-plated, eagle logo pin. 2" x 2". ($100-200) *Courtesy of Dunbar Moonlight Kid Auctions.*

American Motorcyclist Association gave
cloth safety award banners to deserving
motorcycle clubs. 16" x 36". ($50-100)
*Courtesy of Dunbar Moonlight Kid
Auctions.*

American Motorcyclist Association award clock trophy. 1959, 13".
($100-300) *Courtesy of Bob "Sprocket" Eckardt.*

This 1941 American Motorcyclist Association activity contest trophy
was never awarded. 6 1/2" x 4" 11 1/2". ($50-100) *Courtesy of Bob
"Sprocket" Eckardt.*

Chapter 4
A Slice of Hawg Heaven
Harley-Davidson Sales Literature and Paper

The Harley-Davidson motorcycle image—black scuffed leather, skulls, long hair blowing in the wind, "live free or die," spread eagle tattoos, the Grateful Dead, Hell's Angels, Marlon Brando, Peter Fonda, Dennis Hopper, Mary Hart, Jay Leno, Malcolm Forbes, Neil Diamond . . . now, wait just a minute. Who let these last four into the club?

Harley, that's who. Hart, Leno, and Diamond are just three of the many living gems called "rubies" (rich urban bikers) that now adorn Harley's once slightly tarnished but now gleaming chrome crown. (Forbes, unfortunately, is now ordering Dom Perignon in that great biker bar in the sky). Harley's mascot should be a phoenix, not an eagle, because in the last decade, the company's product and image have risen from a pile of ashes big enough to bury a fully dressed Fat Boy.

Harley-Davidson advertising, like its clientele, has come full circle. In the early 1900s, when Harley started its assault on Indian's market share hold, advertising stressed technological advancements (two cylinders instead of one, transmission, headlight, springs, brakes, etc.), smooth riding (ha!), and economy both in purchase price and upkeep against its four-wheeled brethren. With Henry Ford's assembly line accomplishments and subsequent price reductions on the automobile, and a depressed economy following The Great War (I), the few surviving motorcycle companies had to change their pitch.

Schaber's Cycle Shop announced their opening in the 1920s with this flyer. After becoming the world's largest manufacturer of motorcycles in 1918, overtaking Indian, Harley was the place to be. Schaber's, out of New Hampshire, jump-started the new season each year with spring festivities. 5" x 10". ($25-50) *Courtesy of the Dunbar Moonlight Kid Collection.*

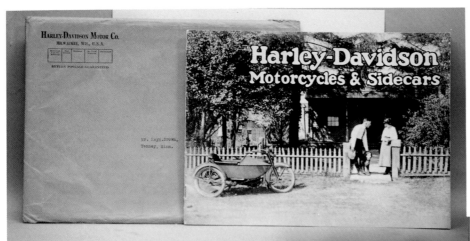

A 1921 Harley-Davidson Catalog. In addition to the countrified cover picturing a sidecar parked in front of a farmhouse, inside were vignettes about people using Harleys. Best of all, though, are full-page illustrated displays of all the year's models with diagrams and cutaways of components. The "V" twin and opposed twin motors are described. In 1921, the company introduced the first "74" JD, which proved quite popular. Even E. Paul DuPont of Indian wrote that he preferred it to his own Indian Big Chief. 33 pages, with mailer, 10 1/2" x 7 1/2" (Rare—100-300) *Courtesy of the Dunbar Moonlight Kid Collection.*

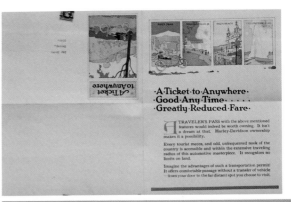

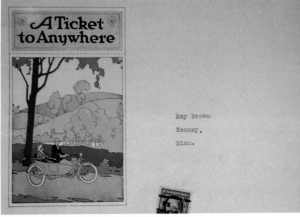

The early 1920s saw a postwar depression that helped to sink cycle sales. Harley production in 1921 was half of 1920, with only 10,000 units made. To rekindle the cycling spirit, Harley advertised "comfort, speed, and cost" as qualities potential buyers would appreciate in their products. This 1922 "A Ticket to Anywhere" brochure was an invitation to use your Harley to "Travel the Harley-Davidson Way." 8 1/2" x 5 1/2". ($30-100) *Courtesy of the Dunbar Moonlight Kid Collection.*

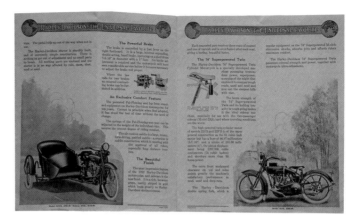

Harley first offered the sidecar in 1914. The following year, motor-cycles were authorized for mail delivery. By 1919, every seven out of ten motorcycles were sidecar models. Harley sent almost all sidecar cycles to the front during World War I. This 1922 Harley-Davidson sales catalog features both the new, beefy "74" solo and the Harley Sidecar, plus single, twin "V", and horizontally opposed-twin type motors, a generator ignition system, two different sidecars, and package delivery. 11 ages, 4" x 9" ($50-200) *Courtesy of he Dunbar Moonlight Kid Collection.*

In 1922, Roy Brown got this packet of information from a Harley-Davidson dealer encouraging him to purchase A "Demon-strator" & Earn His Bike By Selling Others." The packet includes an order form, price list, return envelope, and the original mailing envelope from the dealer. Both Indian and Harley relied heavily on advertising, both in trade and mainstream publications such as the *Saturday Evening Post,* as well as colorful literature designed to please the eye. ($10-40) *Courtesy of the Dunbar Moonlight Kid Collection.*

In 1923, this Harley-Davidson sales aid book helped in the company's campaign to promote the economy and excitement of two-wheeled travel. Selling points included getting eighty miles to the gallon. The dealer book reflects the sporting image Harley wanted to create along with the outdoors passion of its four founders, plugging the joys of taking your Harley fishing, swimming, hunting, and touring. 30 pages, 9" x 12". (Rare—100-300) *Courtesy of Dunbar Moonlight Kid Auctions.*

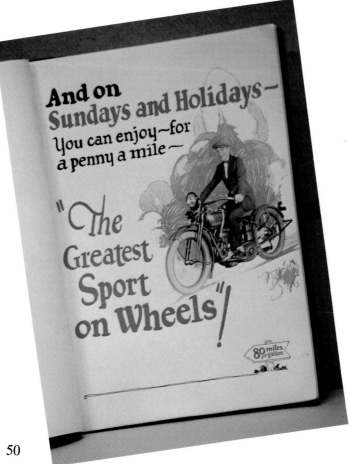

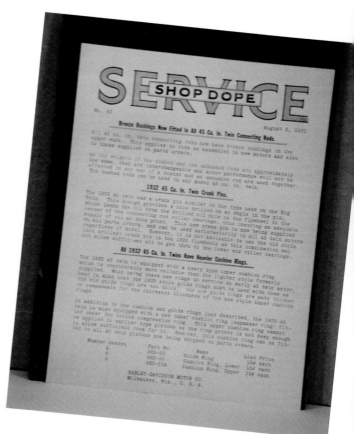

A Quick Ride to Work—

1 Hour

vs.

20 Minutes

and the saving over automobile travel is fully 6 cents per mile!

80 miles per gallon

Swimming—

80 miles per gallon

Touring—

80 miles per gallon

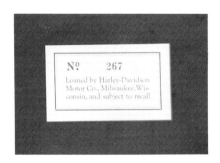

1920 Harley-Davidson *Directory of Spare Parts Catalog* with illustrated parts listings. 90 pages, 6" x 9". ($30-100) *Courtesy of Dunbar Moonlight Kid Auctions.*

Harley-Davidson *Directory of Spare Parts, 1913-1921,* printed in 1923 for Harley motorcycles and sidecars, twin cylinder, heavy weight models. Includes many photos of Harley parts. 93 pages, 6" x 9". ($30-100) *Courtesy of the Dunbar Moonlight Kid Collection.*

Early on motorcycle companies recognized the value of accessories, both for the protection and comfort of their customers and the cash flow created for both producer and dealer. Harley created extensive catalogs featuring clothing, parts, and all kinds of service accessories,. No other company ever marketed its ancillary products as extensively as Harley, which is one reason they are still number one today. This 1920 Harley-Davidson accessories catalog is heavily illustrated, showing tools, lighting, seats, clothing, and oil—an excellent early reference book. 117 pages, 6" x 9". (Rare, $75-200) *Courtesy of Dunbar Moonlight Kid Auctions.*

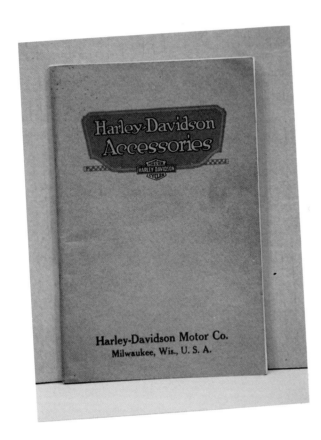

In the 1920s, Harley hailed the fact that its bikes could get 80 miles to the gallon. More importantly, for the flapper class, the company offered its cycles as the perfect companion to outdoor sports, from hunting and fishing to swimming and camping. And motorcycling was a sport in itself, a way to tour the country without glass and steel restraints. Notice all the catalog covers from the 1920s—sidecar bikes with natty, happy couples (this was still pre-helmet era) all alone rolling through the countryside, a promise of a picnic and maybe a little romance around the turn ahead. And Harley has always promoted its cycles to women, although most of the time you'll find women in the sidecar or buddy seat.

In Harley's extensive yearly accessories catalogs, both men and women could find the perfect touring outfits, from protective (and fashionable) black leather jackets and pants, boots, goggles, riding caps, and later, helmets, to a garage full of gadgets, oils, and paints to keep the chrome gleaming and the engine steaming. Often, even today, Harley dealers have made more money from accessory sales than from bike sales.

This style of mainstream marketing, through catalogs and posters dominated Harley's message that everyone, from minor rebel Eddie Haskell to mom June Cleaver, could enjoy life more on a Harley. Unfortunately, such incidents as the 1947 Hollister, California, riots which first gave rise to the Hell's Angels legacy, the 1950s Brando image of *The Wild Ones* (by the way, he rode a Triumph), and excessive rowdiness at national bike meets punched a couple of black eyes into the wholesome image Harley worked so hard to create.

No one really ever stopped loving Harleys—it's just that they started to turn into your neighbor's unpredictable son, the one with the cigarette pack rolled up in his sleeve. Harley has even used that 1960s, *Easy Rider* image in some of its posters to promote its independent hipness while at the same time trying to soften the image of the biker as an outlaw. This has been a very fine line to weave. After being taken over in the 1970s by the Federation of American Motorcyclists, the bowling ball and RV people, (couldn't you just see lefty bowler Earl Anthony in crew cut and plaid polyester on the back of a Sportster?) in 1981, thirteen Harley executives, including great grandson William G. (Willie G.) Davidson, bought back the company and began the reinvention of the Harley image.

Harley sidecars were so popular that left-hand bodies were first exported to the British market in 1917. In the 1920s, sales literature was translated into Spanish, German, and Japanese. "The Open Road Calls You!" in this 1923 Harley-Davidson sales catalog featuring all the 1923 models. 11 pages, 8" x 9" open. ($75-200) *Courtesy of Dunbar Moonlight Kid Auctions.*

While sales at home continued to slump, Harley rumbled overseas with a network of dealers in more than sixty countries. In 1924, more than 6,000 of the 13,000 machines produced were exported. The discontinued small Sport Twin, never a hit in the United States, was popular abroad. This 1924 Harley-Davidson sales brochure features all the 1924 models. 11 pages, 8" x 9" open. ($75-200) *Courtesy of Dunbar Moonlight Kid Auctions.*

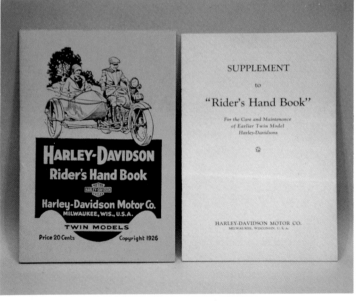

In 1926, Harley published the *Rider's Handbook* and a supplement. 36 pages. ($25-100) *Courtesy of Dunbar Moonlight Kid Auctions*

Harley's hot new model, the 21 ci Peashooter, premiered in 1925, selling much better than Indian's comparable 1926 offering, the Prince. It's featured in this 1925 sales catalog, which touts "Outdoors Greatest Sport." Features inside cover the factory and corporate founders. 11 pages, 8" x 9" open. ($75-200) *Courtesy of Dunbar Moonlight Kid Auctions.*

The mid-twenties saw a number of engineering improvements—the addition of front brakes, improved oil circulation and lubrication, all for a more reliable and pleasant cycling experience. The center spread of the 1926 Harley-Davidson sales catalog focuses on the sidecar. 15 pages, 8" x 9" open. ($75-200) *Courtesy of Dunbar Moonlight Kid Auctions.*

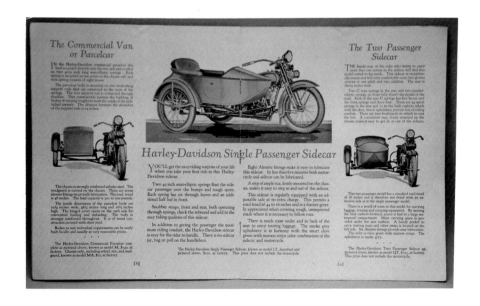

In the past thirteen years, from a 1984 low when you could buy stock for as little as three dollars a share, the cigarette pack has been replaced with Perrier, the T-shirt with a power tie. America's middle and upper classes discovered Harley's heavier, fancier styling and decided the best way to take out their professional frustrations was to unshackle themselves on back roads weekend trips (just like bygone eras). Harley has redefined hip.

Once considered the bike for aspiring rebels and rabble rousers, now attorneys, doctors, and other societal pillars are parking brand new Harleys next to their Volvos and Grand Cherokees, just the kinds of riders Harley has been wooing since the 1920s. Celebrities like Hart and Diamond, among many others, take their Harleys on cross-country trips with full entourages, not to mention saddle bags. This new wave of well-to-do Harley groupies, fueled by an improved motorcycle and brilliant marketing strategy, has helped to propel the company back to the top of the biking world.

We now have the Harley-Davidson Cafe in New York City, home of hipness. We can wear Harley on any part of our body in any manner, thanks to the Harley mail order catalog. A Harley decorated jukebox will only set you back about $8,000, a Harley pinball machine $3,500-$4,500. Daytona, Sturgis, and Laconia still have their annual biker get-togethers and races, and thousands roll into town. But when they leave, the town's coffers are full, not their jail cells.

Harley-Davidson is kicking some serious biking butt in the new-bike sales market. Daily production is up to an average of more than 400 units per day. Harley wants to hold on to its share of more than two thirds of the American market.

What does this mean for those of us who want to invest in Harley memorabilia? Will the market take a sudden dive, just like those wonderful collector cars of the late 1980s whose prices were manipulated until they hit the stratosphere and then crashed into the back door of the vault? Or will the motorcycle memorabilia market continue to soar like a smooth-running Electra Glide?

Harley-Davidson's 1927 fold-out sales catalog was sixteen color pages of singles, twins, sidecars, and parcel cars. Harley mined whatever niche of the market it could, from police forces to commerical transportation, from exports to accessories, in order to augment the civilian business. ($75-200) *Courtesy of the Dunbar Moonlight Kid Collection.*

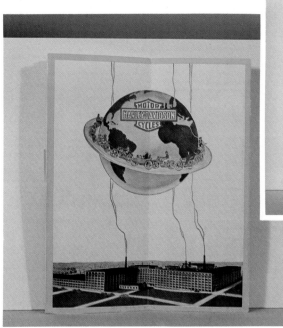

Although still promoting the sport of cycling, by 1929, more than 2,900 police departments had purchased Harleys. This is the year that Harley made double bullet headlights standard and improved the electrical system. Although heading into The Depression, the company still sold more than 20,000 units. Harley-Davidson 1929 sales catalog, 16 pages. ($75-200) *Courtesy of the Dunbar Moonlight Kid Collection.*

Harley turned to bright art deco colors and styles to lure buyer's eyes to their 1930s sales literature. This brochure, "The Sport of A Thousand Joys," is an eleven-page color announcement of the year's models. The action centerfold illustrates "The Greatest Sport of Them All." 8" x 9 1/2". ($50-150) *Courtesy of Dunbar Moonlight Kid Auctions.*

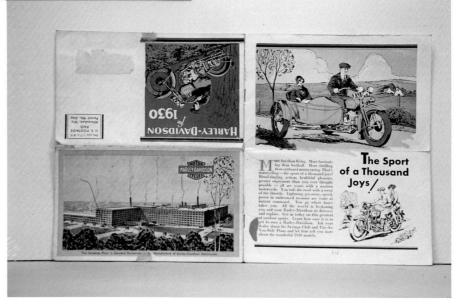

A 1928 Harley-Davidson spare parts catalog illustrates mechanical and sheet metal parts from 1922–28, 82 pages, 6" x 9". ($30-75) *Courtesy of Dunbar Moonlight Kid Collection.*

"New" and "improved" were the buzz words for Indian and Harley in 1930, as seen in this fold-out mailer advertising singles, twins, and sidecars. Most importantly, it showed off the new Big Twin, with new drop-forged forks, interchangeable wheels, and improved clutch. This is the year William H. Davidson won sixth in the grueling Jack Pine Enduro race, wearing a tie. 18" x 9" unfolded. ($30-100) *Courtesy of the Dunbar Moonlight Kid Collection.*

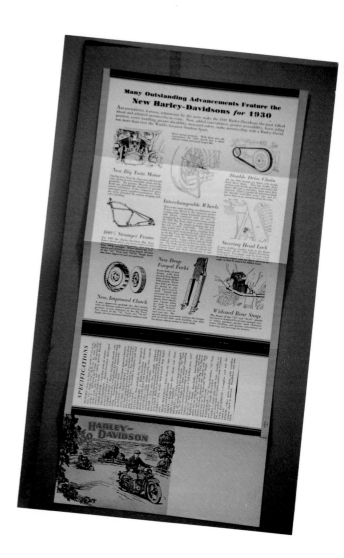

The sales dropoff, both at home and abroad, was felt beginning with the 1931 season. Police contracts became more important and Harley started a controversial direct-sales promotion to police departments that cut into dealer commissions. 1931 Harley-Davidson brochure, 18" x 9" unfolded. ($50-150) *Courtesy of the Dunbar Moonlight Kid Collection.*

Fobs, goggles, clothing, tools, paints, etc., are featured in the 1931 Harley-Davidson spring and summer accessories catalog. 24 Pages. ($50-100) *Courtesy of the Dunbar Moonlight Kid Collection.*

The answer, I think, lies in demographics. Between 1946 and 1967, more than seventy-seven million American consumers were born. These boomers, particularly men who comprise ninety-five percent of Harley buyers, have been increasingly growing not only older, but wealthier and better educated, with a current average age of thirty nine. Only half of the male boomers have reached their forties, and by the year 2010, nearly 25 million of them will still be under sixty. Median income is currently $33,000, up from the $17,000 of ten years ago. Twenty-nine percent have college degrees, up from fourteen percent in 1984. These are the consumers that advertisers drool over.

And, not only are the American boomers taken with Harleys, the world market wants them as well. After losing ground to imports, Harley is now fighting back in Japan, with a marketing campaign capitalizing on its American image, which the Japanese love. Ads in Japan feature American images interposed over Japanese ones—American riders passing a geisha in a rickshaw, Japanese ponies nibbling at a Harley motorcycle. Waiting lists for Harleys in Japan are as long as six months.

Harley has also sponsored HOGs (Harley Owners Groups) in Europe and Japan so that riders can get to know one another and form the same type of fraternity that has been nurtured in the United States since the inception of Harley in 1903. Harley dealerships at home and abroad are also working to educate their riders through open houses and lectures, joining together one big Hog-tied family.

The trickle-down effect into collectibles is inevitable. We boomers love trinkets of history—why else would the Flintstones, Elvis, Hot Wheels, and Mickey Mouse be so popular? Harley, through careful marketing, backed up by a quality product, has inspired a "Let's Go America" mind set that can be purchased through Harley posters, catalogs, brochures, signs, clocks, oil cans, and anything else featuring the black and orange bar and shield logo.

The most difficult challenge, like the new cycle market itself, is finding enough items to meet demand, which is continually growing with no sign of slowing down any time soon. Maybe you were foresighted enough to buy stock in the early 1980s, or you have some nice vintage Harley memorabilia lying around the garage. Maybe you opened a Harley dealership and now bleed black and orange (drip a bit of gold). Almost anyone who has jumped on the Harley-Davidson rock 'n' roll bandwagon before it hit full stride has been amply rewarded for their patronage.

So, unless the NASA program progresses so quickly that we're speeding about in George Jetson-type space coasters in the near future, riding the Harley-Davidson market means cruising down one big open road with all points of the globe stretching far ahead.

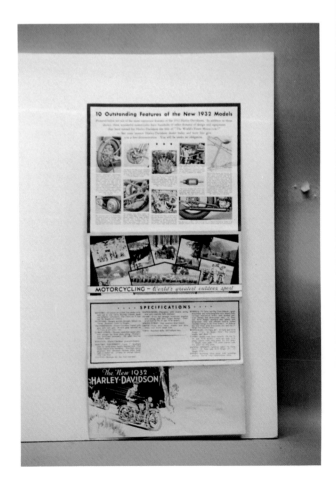

In the 1932 fold-out Harley sales brochure, six new models are graphically presented with their outstanding features. Clean-cut riders in action grace the cover. 9" x 18" unfolded. ($30-100) *Courtesy of the Dunbar Moonlight Kid Collection.*

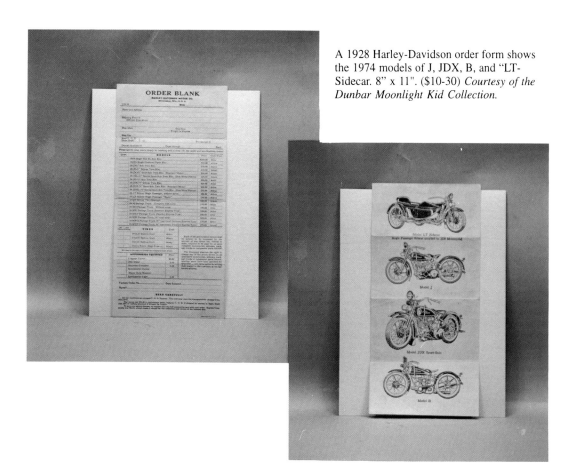

A 1928 Harley-Davidson order form shows
the 1974 models of J, JDX, B, and "LT-
Sidecar. 8" x 11". ($10-30) *Courtesy of the
Dunbar Moonlight Kid Collection.*

Thirty-one pages of vintage Harley add-on and replacement
merchandise plus clothing can be found in this 1935 Harley-
Davidson Accessories Catalog. 6" x 9". ($50-100) *Courtesy of the
Dunbar Moonlight Kid Collection.*

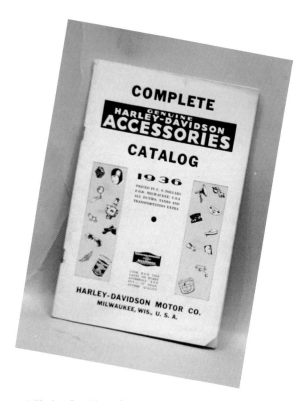

A Harley-Davidson Genuine Accessories Catalog from 1936 has
thirty-one pages of vintage Harley add-on and replacement merchandise and clothing. 6" x 9". ($50-100) *Courtesy of the Dunbar
Moonlight Kid Collection.*

The year 1937 proved to be Harley's best during The Depression, with sales of more than 11,000 cycles. Strapped for cash, Harley was still able to introduce a 61-ci ohv model (aka the Knucklehead, which was made until 1947), an "80" side valve, and also to make improvements in the four-speed gearbox. This 1937 Harley-Davidson sales booklet features models "45" Twin, "61" Twin, "74" Twin, "80" Twin and Sidecar, Package Truck and Servi-Car. 11 pages, 6" x 9". ($25-100) *Courtesy of the Dunbar Moonlight Kid Collection.*

The black-and-white cover of the 1937 Harley-Davidson *Modern Accessories for the Motorcyclist* catalog shows couple riding "buddy" on a "37" Harley. In total, there are 31 pages featuring genuine clothing and merchandise, 6" x 9". ($50-100) *Courtesy of the Dunbar Moonlight Kid Collection*

A traffic cop helps plug the Harley radio equipped police special "Used all over the world" in this 1939 sales brochure. 8 1/2" x 11 1/2". ($30-100) *Courtesy of Dunbar Moonlight Kid Auctions.*

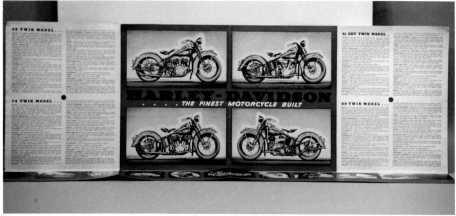

The epitome of the clean-cut, uniformed motorcycle rider—the opposite of Marlon Brando in *The Wild Ones*--is depicted on this Harley sales-service envelope from Scranton, Pennsylvania. ($5-25).*Courtesy of the Dunbar Moonlight Kid Collection,*

The Harley 125 Lightweight was the first new model introduced by the company after World War II. Originally it was designed by German engineers. However, Germany lost all patent rights in World War II, so the cycle was made for five years in America. Harley 125 double-sided sales brochure, circa 1948, 7" x 10". ($10-40) *Courtesy of the Dunbar Moonlight Kid Collection.*

Harley's sales brochure shows all new models in candid photos, like this one of a smiling couple riding "buddy" on the cover. The Panhead debuted in 1948, had hydraulic front forks installed in 1949, and a foot shift in 1952. This model continued as the Hydra-Glide and Duo-Glide and finished in 1954 as the Electra Glide, one of Harley's most popular models. 12 pages, 8" x 6". ($20-50) *Courtesy of the Dunbar Moonlight Kid Collection.*

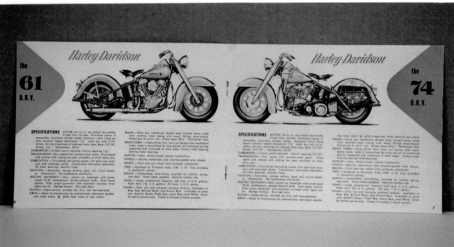

Harley-Davidson took a fun theme for its 1951, 15-page sales catalog. The company brought more horses that year—fifty-five of them—to the Panhead series. ($20-50) *Courtesy of the Dunbar Moonlight Kid Collection.*

1954 Special Golden 50th Anniversary
Harley-Davidson genuine parts and
accessories catalog had 37 pages with
celebratory clothes, saddlebags, and
emblems. ($50-100) *Courtesy of the
Dunbar Moonlight Kid Collection.*

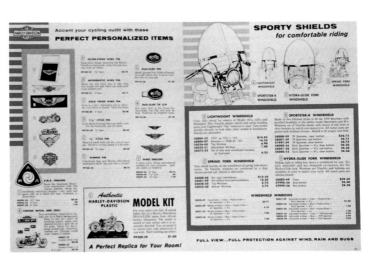

The 1959 Harley-Davidson accessory catalog had 35 pages of
accessories, paints, oil, tools, pins, and other necessities. ($30-75)
Courtesy of Dunbar Moonlight Kid Auctions.

The *Harley-Davidson Rider Accessories Catalog* was very well illustrated with clothing, show-and-go add-ons, pre-luxe oils, etc. 1963, 31 pages, 8" x 11". ($20-75) *Courtesy of the Dunbar Moonlight Kid Collection.*

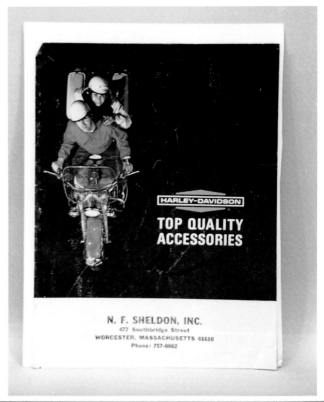

In 1981, Harley commemorated the company's re-establishment of Harley-Davidson after its buyout from AMF, the bowling ball and recreational vehicle company. This momento is signed by Vaughn Beals and Charles Thompson. 9" x 12". ($20-50) *Courtesy of the Dunbar Moonlight Kid Collection.*

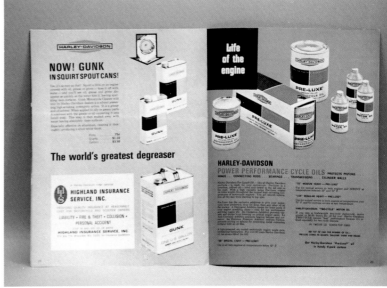

The 1965 Harley-Davidson *Factory Accessories & Cycling Smart Wear Catalog* helped sell tools, paint, and pre-luxe motor oil in addition to the new 1966 models. ($30-75) *Courtesy of the Dunbar Moonlight Kid Collection.*

Chapter 5
Smoke Signals from Wigwam
Indian Motocycles Sales Literature and Paper

In a pre-World War United States, the Indian Motocycle was the hottest selling, fastest riding, best marketed, most brilliantly engineered motorcycle in the world. Somehow, four decades later, the company's product fell from "Standard of the World" down to a cruel joke. The Wigwam folded up and the site truly became the home of the "Silent Indian."

When a talented creator and a creative entrepreneur meet and share the same passion, that's when a business is born. George M. Hendee raced high-wheeled bicycles in the 1880s, winning more than 300 races in a four-year stretch. Oscar Hedstrom raced bicycles professionally, then, as safety bicycles passed their high-wheeled counterparts in popularity, produced a motorized pacing bicycle for board track racing. The two met in Springfield, Massachusetts, and Hedstrom signed an agreement to develop a new-fangled motorized bicycle, an "Indian Motocycle." The name was chosen in honor of the American native and "motocycle" as Hendee remembered the winning term from a newspaper contest to rename the phrase "horseless carriage."

With Oscar Hedstrom's engineering brilliance and George Hendee's flair for marketing, Indian dominated both the worldwide motorcycle market and the racetrack through the early part of this century. In 1908, the company offered the first racer in its catalog, with a diamond frame, and in 1909, Indian introduced a loop frame to customers. Committed to racing, the Hendee Company joined forces with promoter Jack Prince and built a 1/3-mile circular motordrome in Indian's hometown, Springfield, Massachusetts, which was probably the inspiration for this cover. This 1909 Indian Motocycles Catalog is a very early and very rare catalog. ($150-600) *Courtesy of the Dunbar Moonlight Kid Collection.*

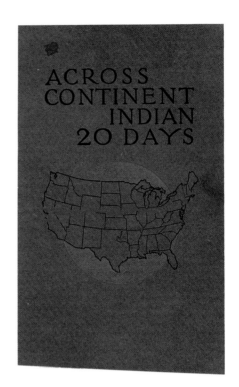

Although the Hendee company offered the loop frame in its 1909 catalog, buyers could still purchase twins with diamond frames until stock ran out. The standard Indian color up until 1911 was royal blue, though vermillion, or Indian red, was an option. *Courtesy of the Dunbar Moonlight Kid Collection.*

Indian was probably at its zenith in 1911. By the end of the year, Indian owned every amateur and professional speed and distance record—121 in all. Indian riders placed first, second, and third in the prestigious Isle of Man Tourist Trophy, including a second place for Irishman Charles B. Franklin, who later joined the Indian Motocycle Company as an engineer. Oliver C. Godfey won, and A. J. Moorehouse placed third. Indian advertising booklet, *Across the Continent on an Indian in 20 Days*, 1911. ($50-200) *Courtesy of the Dunbar Moonlight Kid Collection.*

On June 26, 1911, Volney Davis left San Fransisco on his Indian twin, endeavoring to set a new transcontinental record. Twenty days, 9 hours, and 11 minutes later, he appeared in New York, setting a new record and adding to the growing Indian legend. *Courtesy of the Dunbar Moonlight Kid Collection.*

In 1901, Hedstrom finished three machines. By the time Hedstrom retired in 1913, at the age of 43, Indian had smoked the competition, becoming the largest manufacturer of motorcycles in the world, producing 32,000 motorcycles that year and bringing in profits of $1.3 million (well over a hundred million dollars in 1997 terms). Vermillion Indian ads decorated the covers of motorcycling magazines such as *Motorcycling* and *Motorcycle Illustrated*. Indian dominated the new breed of motorcycle endurance races, tourist trophy races, hill climbs, and board track races, leaving hundreds of imitators and competitors choking on exhaust.

Improvements illustrated in early Indian sales catalogs feature the introduction of the twist-grip throttle in 1905; speedier twin cylinder models in 1907; changeover from the traditional bicycle diamond frame to a loop frame in 1909; a new leaf-spring fork in 1910; powerful eight-valve twins in 1911, and the cradle-spring frame in 1913. Little is known about who exactly created and developed Indian's advertising and sales literature campaigns. As president, it can be assumed that George Hendee had much to do with the marketing. Companies like Indian had to rely on print and visual advertising to push first-time buyers through the door. Once they were sold, then they would be pulled back by the positive experience of riding an Indian.

More so than the other two members of the Big Three (Harley-Davidson and Excelsior), Indian pushed the thrill of riding with its spectacular color litho catalog covers, particularly in the late teens. Introducing its trademark Indian red color in 1909, the covers alone excited the eye of the potential customer.

Inside, those who were technologically inspired could read about the qualities of Indian bikes, the thrills provided, and how the chore of transportation could be transformed into a pleasure, all for a fraction of an automobile's cost. The beauty of these catalogs culminates in the litho image series from 1915-1919, with an oil-painting quality to the artistry, including those catalogs created in 1918-19, the war years.

It is easy to deduce, then, that the earliest and most dynamic sales literature, posters, and brochures are the rarest, the most desirable, and usually the most valuable. (Note—A number of these catalogs have been reproduced beautifully. If you are not experienced in purchasing literature, make sure you know or receive a guarantee from the person who is selling the piece to you.) Original catalogs from this era are worth $100-$800 each, depending on condition. Posters are rarer and can run into the thousands.

Riders often had to be their own mechanics, so this Indian Price List was almost as valuable in 1911 as it is today. The book lists all diamond-frame models up to 1909 and includes some photo pages. 96 pages, 3 1/2" x 6 1/4". ($50-150) *Courtesy of the Dunbar Moonlight Kid Collection.*

Early parts books like these are scarce and valuable resources, particularly for those with early, restorable Indians. 1912 Price List Book #12 for parts from 1909–1912, loop-frame models only, stamped William T. Hulse, 250 pages, 4" x 7". ($50-150) *Courtesy of the Dunbar Moonlight Kid Collection.*

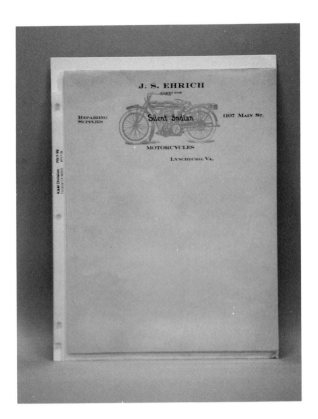

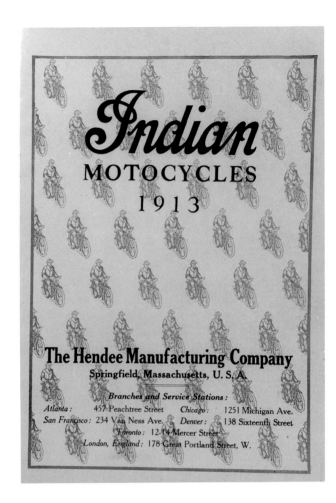

"Silent Indian" dealer stationery with early motorcycle, circa 1912, 8 1/2" x 11". (Rare—50-100) *Courtesy of the Dunbar Moonlight Kid Collection.*

At various times, a number of motorcycle makers, including the "big three" (Indian, Excelsior, and Harley) relied on exports for a portion of their operating profits. Indian even had a factory for a short while in Toronto, Canada, in the early teens, as well as a showroom in that city. *Courtesy of the Dunbar Moonlight Kid Collection.*

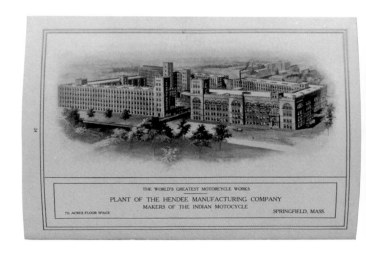

With profits of more than $1.3 million on sales of 32,000 cycles, 1913 was Indian's biggest year ever. Indian had grown so big and so successful that Oscar Hedstrom chose this time to take his profits and retire, the end of Indian's most golden era. This 1913 Indian Motocycles Sales Catalog was offered by a dealer who called himself The Motorcycle Man. ($100-600) *Courtesy of the Dunbar Moonlight Kid Collection.*

Site of the Wigwam, as the Indian Motocycle factory was affectionately called. This 1913 rendering shows the factory at full capacity. By the 1930s, only five percent of its available space was being used. *Courtesy of the Dunbar Moonlight Kid Collection.*

The Indian logo, circa 1913. The story goes that Hendee and Hendstrom chose the name Indian because theirs was the first native motorcycle of the country. Forty-odd years after Indian's demise, the logo still stands for engineering and beauty.

This 1913 Indian Motocycles operation manual includes how-to infomation along with specifics on mechanical systems, singles and twins, and some do's and don'ts. ($50-150) *Courtesy of the Dunbar Moonlight Kid Collection.*

Early Indian Motocycle postcard shows bike with an oversize headlight and posed driver. ($20-50) *Courtesy of the Dunbar Moonlight Kid Collection.*

The back cover of the 1913 Indian catalog. *Courtesy of the Dunbar Moonlight Kid Collection.*

Motorcycle postcard shows three bikes lined up with two drivers. The bike on the left is an Indian, the two others are to be determined. ($20-50) *Courtesy of the Dunbar Moonlight Kid Collection.*

As a result of Indian's great victories in the Isle of Man and Brooklands races and Cannonball Baker's touring Down Under, Indians were very popular in England and Australia. *Courtesy of the Dunbar Moonlight Kid Collection.*

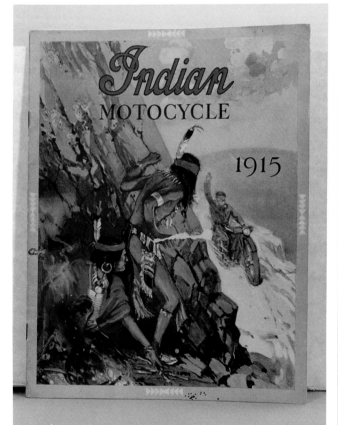

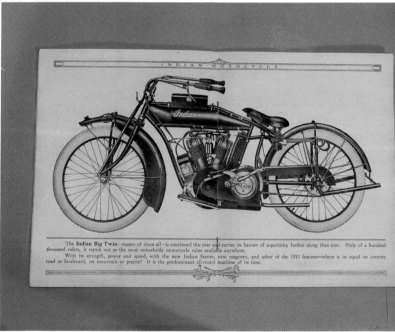

The cover of this 1915 Indian Motocycle Catalog tells it all. Will the two scouts make peace with the adventurous rider? Or, will he be pushed off the edge? There were signs that Indian's fortunes might be changing. George Hendee followed his former partner into retirement. The Great War was invading Europe. This was to be the last year of Hedstrom's F-head, or pocket valve engines. Sales were still relatively strong at 21,000 in 1915, but down from 25,000 in 1914. ($100-500) *Courtesy of the Dunbar Moonlight Kid Collection.*

Indian's Big Twin for 1915. Although not shown here, options included an electric starter, three-speed transmission, electric lights, and generator. Indian was fighting for market share against both Harley-Davidson and the exploding growth of the auto industry. *Courtesy of the Dunbar Moonlight Kid Collection.*

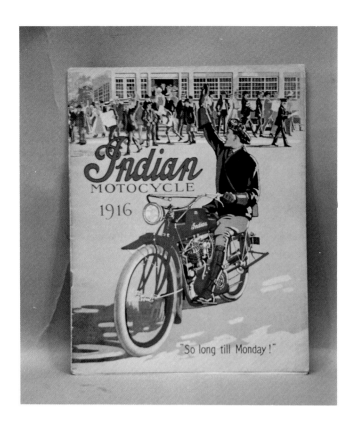

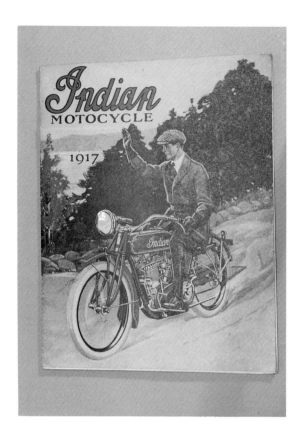

Indian's early color and graphics, as seen on this 1916 catalog, could make Harley look like a silent and dull-grey fellow. This catalog marks a change in the direction of motorcycle advertising, from transportation to sport vehicle to help justify the pricetag. Motorcycling wasn't about getting from point A to point B anymore, it was about enjoying the ride in between. The centerfold touts new innovations in the Cradle Spring Frame. Models advertised include Model "F" Solo, Model F Indian Sidecar, Model "K" Featherweight, Models "F, G, K & H", Model H in racing configuration, and parcel car. Also, there are sectioned schematics of the "power plus" motor, three-speed transmission, and the two-stroke motor and transmission assembly. 24 pages, 8" x 10". ($100-500) *Courtesy of the Dunbar Moonlight Kid Collection.*

The most noticeable change for the Powerplus in 1917 was the new rounded, more stylish, and, surprisingly, cheaper-to-make fuel tank. Indian entered into military contracts for World War I, contracts that would net them short-term profits and ultimately scalp their long-term ties with dealers. With heightened military orders, Indian ignored civilian orders, so dealers, facing no stock for their customers, turned their allegiance to a ready and willing Harley-Davidson. 1917 Indian Motocycle Catalog. ($100-500) *Courtesy of the Dunbar Moonlight Kid Collection.*

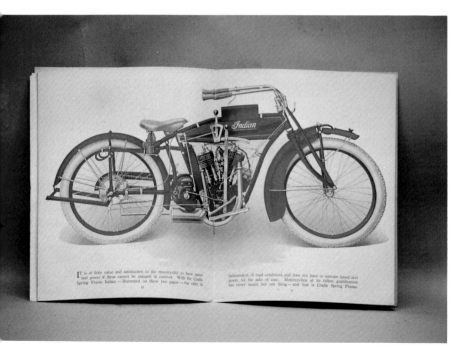

Centerfold of 1916 catalog.

For instance, in 1909 the Wigwam produced almost 5,000 motorcycles. How many of these sales catalogs featuring an explosive board track racer (Jake DeRosier?) could have been printed? For a fledging industry, with a brand new network of dealers, how many copies were distributed? How many survived? Before the days of mass media, catalogs were always passed from hand to hand, to be studied and used for entertainment. How many pairs of soiled hands could these have gone through before they were sent out with the Sears catalog?

How about posters? Would they automatically come down with the new season, with new models, with new improvements? The inherent fragility of paper makes it amazing that posters, catalogs, and brochures survived at all.

Although Oscar Hedstrom retired in 1913 at the age of 43, Charles Gustafson, a former champion motorcycle racer, created a whole new line of Indians, the Powerplus series, featuring a newly designed engine. These debuted in the 1916 season, and were given a huge publicity push, thanks to Cannonball Baker's 1915 Three Flags (Canada, the United States, and Mexico) record-setting endurance run.

George M. Hendee retired in 1916, dying at the age of 77 in 1943. Why both men left at relatively young ages is a mystery. Did they feel they had accomplished all they could in this arena and wanted a new challenge? Had they amassed such large fortunes that they did not need to work anymore? Did they foresee a negative change in the wind? The answer is probably all of the above. Hendee worked as a fundraiser for the Shriner's Hospital for Crippled Children and Hedstrom spent his time building championship winning race boats, dying at the age of 90 in 1960.

So how did the world's largest motorcycle manufacturer fall from the golden age? Crooked management, poor business decisions, strong competition, and bad economic times all conspired to take the wahoo out of the whoop.

Following the Powerplus development was the creation of the Scout middleweight motorcycle by Irishman Charles B. Franklin, a former racer and Indian distributor in the United Kingdom, who came over to work as an engineer for Indian in 1916. Franklin's other major claim to fame was Indian's longest-running model, the heavyweight 74" Chief, introduced in 1922.

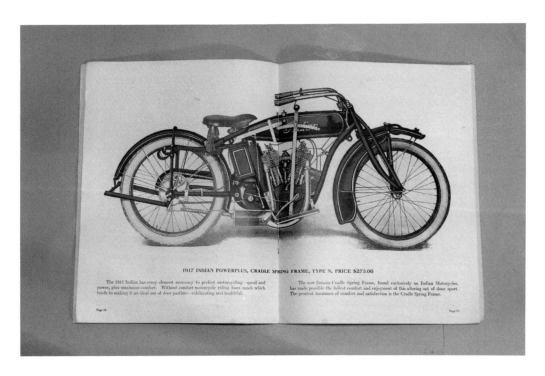

In 1917, this Powerplus could be bought for $275, just about the same price Henry Ford was charging for a Model T. It's no wonder then that automobile sales rose dramatically. *Courtesy of the Dunbar Moonlight Kid Collection.*

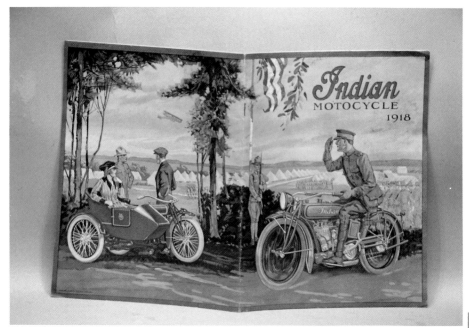

An Army dispatch rider scouts for danger on an Indian, a military camp with troops lies in the background. Inside, the centerfold shows off a type N-18, 1918 Indian Power Plus in color. Other pages contain very detailed descriptions of new models and one page regarding the Indian bicycle. There were only minor changes in the 1918 models: different shaped handlebars, new use of cables, and new levers. In 1918, Indian sold 22,000 units, plus 13,300 sidecar units, mostly to the military. Indian's profits for that year were $733,000, but they came at a high cost. While Indian was playing patriot, Harley-Davidson snuck through the front line at home and made huge inroads into the civilian market share. Indian would never catch up. 1918 Indian Color Catalog, 23 pages. ($100-500) *Courtesy of the Dunbar Moonlight Kid Collection.*

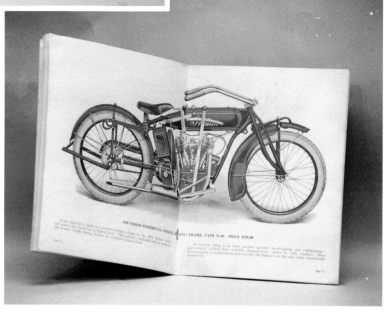

The Scout, possibly Indian's most best loved model, got its start in 1920. Even Goldilocks (during her bike days) would have loved the Scout—it handled great, had plenty of power, and could be ridden by beginners. The 1920 Indian catalog was very similiar to the 1912 edition. Inside it featured Scout Type "G20" and Type "NE 20" in color centerfold and sidecar on a color page. Also Type "W 20" Single Cylinder Commercial Power Plus Specifications and schematics were shown in detail. 24 pages, 8" x 10". *Courtesy of the Dunbar Moonlight Kid Collection.* $100-400

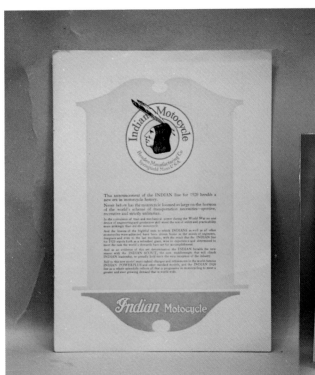

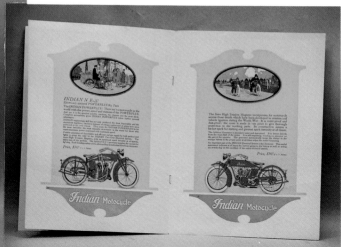

In 1920 Indian issued this eight-page, full-color sales catalog featuring the Scout, Powerplus, Big Twin, Sidecar, and Commercial Parcel Car. The Powerplus was continued until 1922, when it underwent a name change and became the Standard, so as not to confuse it with the new heavyweight Chief model. 9" x 11". ($100-300) *Courtesy of Dunbar Moonlight Kid Collection.*

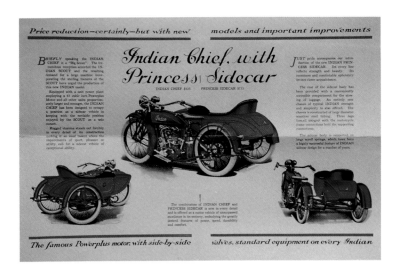

Announcing reduced prices, Indian issued this pamphlet in 1922, featuring Chief with Princess Sidecar, Chief Solo, Scout, and Indian Standard. The New Big Twin Chief with 61 cu inch engine proved to be a huge success for Indian, the big brother to the Scout. However, Indian still only sold half as many motorcycles as Harley in 1922, possibly prompting this announced reduction in prices. 9" x 6". ($75-200) *Courtesy of the Dunbar Moonlight Kid Collection.*

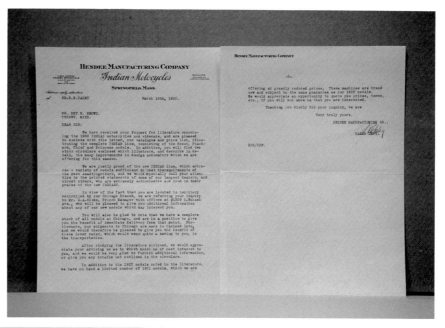

Roy Brown is given a personal invitation to save on reduced-price leftover models in this Hendee/Indian letter that mentions the 1922 catalog. ($10-30) *Courtesy of the Dunbar Moonlight Kid Collection.*

You could take your Chief solo or buy the sidecar version for the Princess of your choice when shopping with this 1922 Indian fold-out brochure. 24" x 12" open. ($50-150) *Courtesy of the Dunbar Moonlight Kid Collection.*

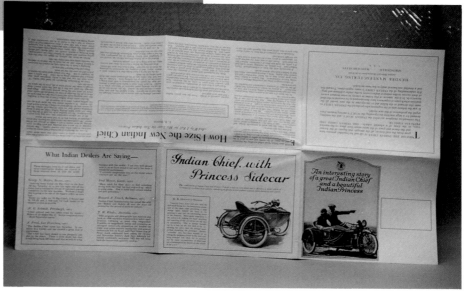

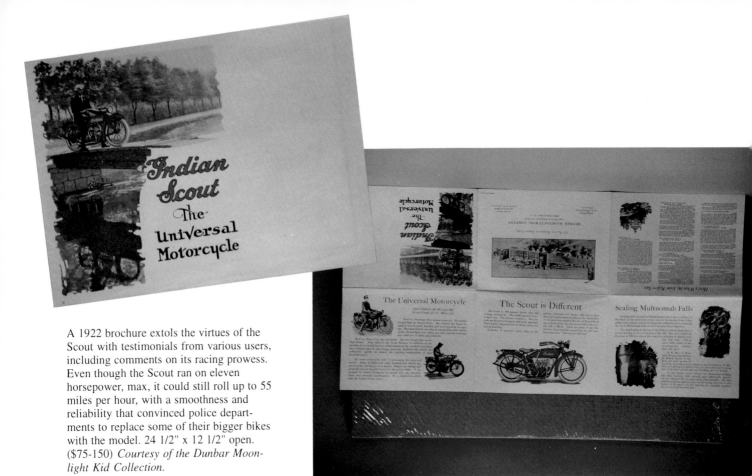

A 1922 brochure extols the virtues of the
Scout with testimonials from various users,
including comments on its racing prowess.
Even though the Scout ran on eleven
horsepower, max, it could still roll up to 55
miles per hour, with a smoothness and
reliability that convinced police departments to replace some of their bigger bikes
with the model. 24 1/2" x 12 1/2" open.
($75-150) *Courtesy of the Dunbar Moon-
light Kid Collection.*

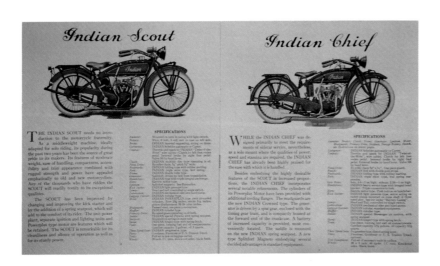

Inside this 1922 brochure, Indian's three
basic models—the Standard, Scout, and the
Chief with and without Princess sidecar—
get a plug, with diagrams of components
and cutaways. Literature of this era stressed
excitement, economy, and dependability. 7
pages, 8" x 9 1/2" open. ($75-150) *Courtesy
of the Dunbar Moonlight Kid Collection.*

Introduced in 1923, Big Chief "74" with Sidecar proved to be even more popular than the the Chief "61" Solo. 1924 Indian sales brochure, 11 pages, 8" x 9". ($50-150) *Courtesy of the Dunbar Moonlight Kid Collection.*

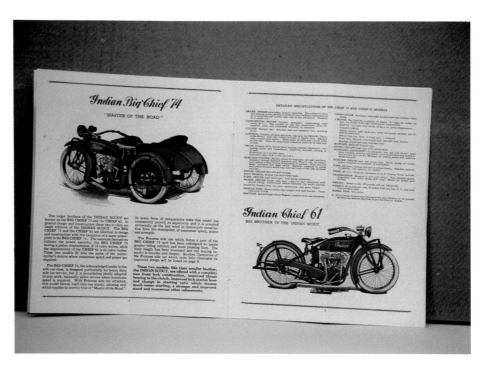

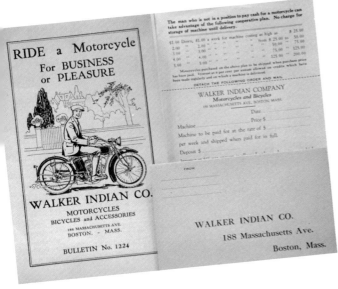

This 1924 Walker Indian Company sales brochure listed used and demonstrator motorcycles for sale. Walker was the distributor for Indian in the Boston area. Illustrated booklet lists a number of makes (including Harley and Excelsior) and models as well as new and used sidecars and accessories. Includes order form and mailing envelope, 5 1/2" x 8 1/2". ($30-100) *Courtesy of the Dunbar Moonlight Kid Collection.*

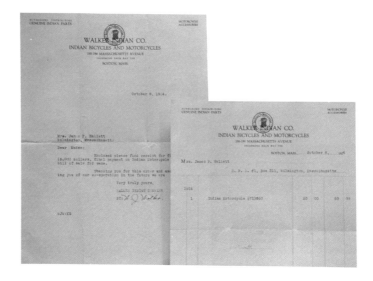

A 1924 Walker Indian Company letter and bill of sale for an unknown model of Indian motorcycle. ($10-30) *Courtesy of the Dunbar Moonlight Kid Collection.*

The catalogs for the 1920s still offer eye-catching color and graphic designs, but in a cost-cutting dimension. Colors are restricted to red, black, and white, a severe drop-off from the palette previously offered. The output of these catalogs was also greater, so the price range on catalogs is in the $75-$300 range, depending on the catalog and condition.

From 1928-31, no new models were offered, so each year the emphasis is on model improvements. This reflects the most volatile and chaotic period as the non-motorcycle enthusiast management spent its time trying to break into the outboard motor, refrigerator, automobile shock, and ventilator industries, with no success. Also, there were some shaky back-room deals going on which robbed the company of much needed capital.

Millionaire E. Paul DuPont rescued Indian in 1930 and brought on Joe Hosely of his DuPont automobile company to take over the Indian helm, getting rid of the corrupt management.

The Prince was introduced in 1926, a small model meant for the entry level rider and export. Unfortunately for Indian, Harley also put out a similar model at the same time and the Prince never sold as well. After two years, Indian stopped production. Therefore, Prince sales literature is hard to find. Information on other models, such as the one-year Motoplane of 1932 and the infamous upside-down Indian 4 series of 1936-37, are also sought after and scarce. One positive thing Indian did in 1927 was to buy the rights to the late William Henderson Ace four-cylinder motorcycle.

It debuted as the Indian Ace Collegiate Four, then later became simply the Indian 4. Again, any of the Indian Ace literature, only used for two years, is also desirable and hard to find.

In the 1930s, Indian's literature was changed to more photo-based layouts. Like Harley brochures, these handouts showed the bike at play. In 1934, the company first displayed its newly opened fenders and also offered twenty-four different paint colors for Indians. These fenders became full-flared skirts in 1940, as shown on the cover of that year's catalog, for some reason colored in lime green. In 1939, influenced by the New York World's Fair, DuPont offered the option of that year's turquoise, orange, and white color scheme.

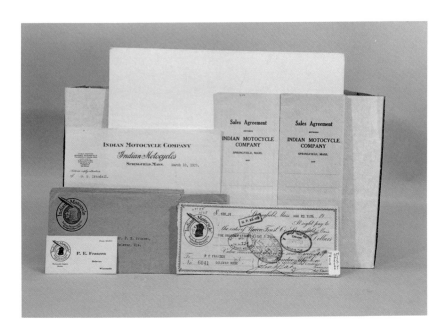

In 1926, the changeover from the Hendee company to Indian Motocycles was complete. Here is an Indian Factory sales agreement dated March 4, 1925, with P. E. Franzen specifying territory and discounts; original sales contract and duplicate sales contract with warranty terms; letter of procedure and terms dated March 10, 1925, Franzen's business card as an Indian dealer; Indian motorcycle's check to P. E. Franzen dated March 23, 1926 for $188.21 with Indian logo and bank cancelling stamp, and the original envelope dated March 10, 1925. Franzen, from Delavan, Wisconsin, was one of the earliest Indian dealers. ($50-150) *Courtesy of Dunbar Moonlight Kid Auctions.*

Like the Chief, riders preferred the larger "45" Scout motor to the "37." An invitation to ride the Indian Scout, circa 1926–28, 5 1/2" x 8". ($25-75) *Courtesy of the Dunbar Moonlight Kid Collection.*

In 1925 the Scout was given balloon tires, a look which gave the bike more volume, shown here in a 1926 fold-out filled with specifications and schematics. 6 pages, 6" x 9". ($50-125) *Courtesy of the Dunbar Moonlight Kid Collection.*

A 1922–1926 *Indian Chief and Sidecar Parts Book*, 98 pages, 6" x 9". ($50-150) *Courtesy of Dunbar Moonlight Kid Auctions.*

A 1920–1925 Indian Motorcyles parts catalog lists every nut and bolt from aero magneto to rear wheels, shown and itemized and priced in this extensive, 120-page catalog with fold-out diagram of clutch, transmission, and Chief motor. A fantastic early reference. 6" x 9". ($50-150) *Courtesy of the Dunbar Moonlight Kid Collection.*

The Big Chief, Indian's biggest seller, proved so much more popular than the Chief, that the "61" version was discontinued in 1930. This 1926 Indian Big Chief "74" fold-out has specifications and schematics. 6 pages, 6" x 9". ($50-125) *Courtesy of the Dunbar Moonlight Kid Collection.*

Indian Motocycle Co sent this Christmas/New Years card in the 1920s featuring their solemn Indian logo with mistletoe. 5 1/4" x 3 1/4". ($30-75) *Courtesy of Dunbar Moonlight Kid Auctions.*

For some reason the "modern magic carpet imagery" did not sway potential buyers of the Prince, introduced in 1925 as a side valve, then changed to an overhead valve in 1926. With a 21-cubic-meter motor, it seemed the model never found its market, either domestically or abroad, and was dropped in 1929. Indian Prince fold-out brochure, 1926, 18" x 9" open. ($50-125) *Courtesy of the Dunbar Moonlight Kid Collection.*

Indian changed the Prince's motor, changed the gas tank, and got a front break, but still couldn't find a loyal following like those the Scout and Big Chief commanded. Indian Prince fold-out brochure, 1928, 9" x 24" open. ($50-125) *Courtesy of the Dunbar Moonlight Kid Collection.*

A valuable listing of interchangeable parts from 1920–28 can be found in this Indian Ace parts catalog, 17 pages, 6" x 9". ($30-100) *Courtesy of Dunbar Moonlight Kid Auctions.*

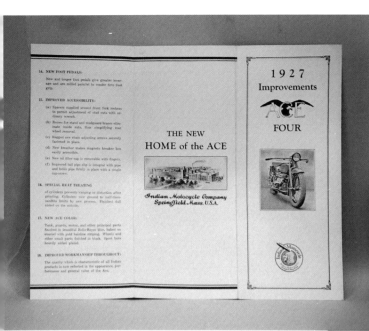

Indian bought the manufacturing rights and tooling to Bill Henderson's Ace in 1927. The Indian Ace became the Indian 4 in 1929. Indian Ace Sales Brochure, 1927, 11" x 19". ($50-150) *Courtesy of the Dunbar Moonlight Kid Collection.*

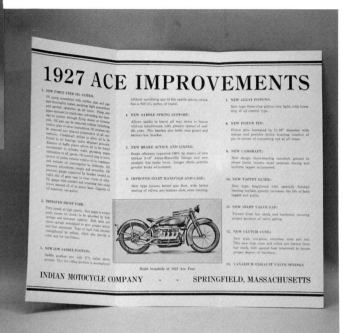

The Indian Ace gave Excelsior-Henderson a run for the four-cylinder market. Bill Henderson sold the rights to his Henderson 4 to Ignaz Schwinn in 1917, then built his all-new Ace cycle, only to be killed in 1922 while test riding one of his cycles. Indian and Ace Motorcycles dealer brochure, 1927, with tagalong ads from other businesses and driving distances from Amsterdam, New York, 10" x 6 1/2" open. ($30-100) *Courtesy of the Dunbar Moonlight Kid Collection.*

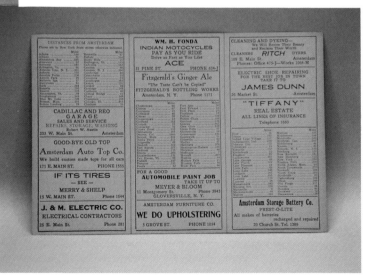

This great little catalog shows the entire Indian lineup, including the Indian Armored Motorcycle used for chasing bootleggers. It also shows that, while Indian still advertised and marketed heavily, the company also made unprofitable investments in non-motorcycle items such as the automobile shock absorbers seen here. Bad investments proved to be one of the reasons for Indian's eventual downfall. Rare-sized Indian "vest pocket" miniature catalog for motorcycles and bicycles, dealer Elmer Wolfe & Sons, 1929, eight pages of different model motorcycles, delivery prices on back cover, 3 1/2" x 2 1/4". ($50-200) *Courtesy of Dunbar Moonlight Kid Auctions.*

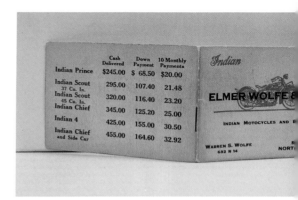

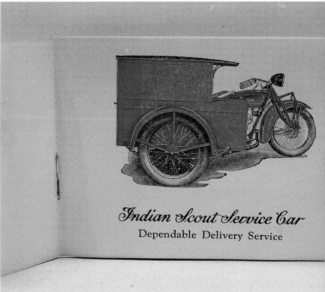

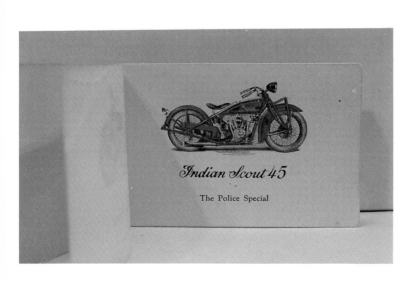

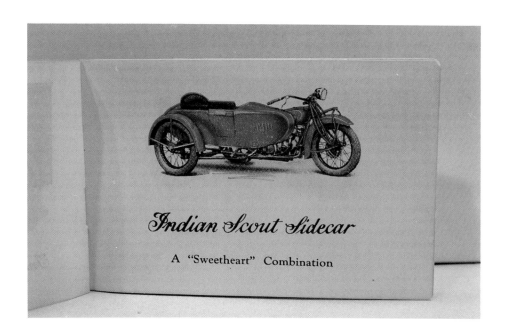

Indian Scout Sidecar

A "Sweetheart" Combination

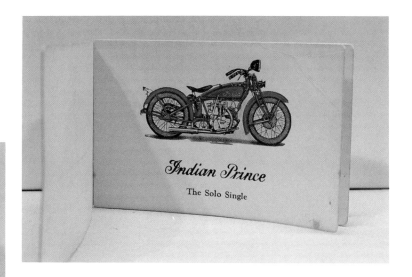

Indian Prince

The Solo Single

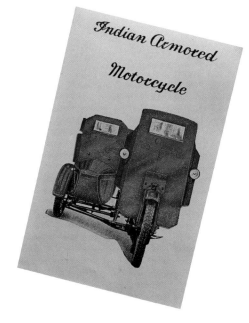

Indian Armored Motorcycle

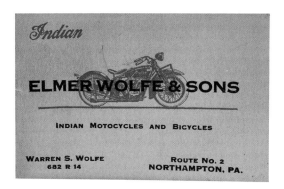

Indian

ELMER WOLFE & SONS

INDIAN MOTOCYCLES AND BICYCLES

WARREN S. WOLFE
682 R 14

ROUTE No. 2
NORTHAMPTON, PA.

E. Paul DuPont spent most of the 1930s trying to boost Indian sales and solve Indian engineering problems and quality control with the Chief models. Fazing out the Scout in 1932, Indian's most popular model, angered its dealers, who were further infuriated with the much more fragile Motoplane replacement.

The posters from this period are very cartoonish, many showing drawings of Indian people, not necessarily the bikes themselves. Occasionally you can find an Indian racing poster, but they are scarcer than their Harley counterparts.

In 1940, Joe Hosely died, in 1942 the United States went to war. the company recovered to show profits in 1942 and 1943, with 16,000 units sold each year, most to the military, but still just over half of Harley sales. For some reason, the curtain came crashing down in 1944, when only 3,800 motorcycles were made. The company never recovered. Literature from this period is tough to find. As during World War I, most of Indian's total output was for military sales, with no new models.

In 1945, E. Paul DuPont, tired of the endless struggle, sold out to an investment group headed by Ralph B. Rogers. He in turn, brought on G. Briggs Weaver, an Indian de-

signer of the 1930s who created the flared fender line, to develop a series of lightweight and middleweight motorcycles for the Torque Manufacturing Company of Connecticut, soon to move to the Wigwam, Indian's manufacturing plant in Springfield, Mass. Indian reorganized, got financing, and prepared for a brand new era.

Rogers hit the road and doubled the number of Indian dealers, from 450 to nearly 900. He also designed a marketing campaign aimed toward the new middle class, the same one that was building families, buying houses in the suburbs, and filling those homes with all sorts of great time-saving appliances. Rogers brought sports and movie stars to the literature to promote the motorcycles. Everything was in place for a big Indian comeback. . . .

If only the quality of the motorcycles had been as good as the plan, Indian might have been able to ride out the final storm. Unfortunately, the craftsmanship in the manufacture of the parts and the piecing together of the new line of Arrow and Warrior bikes was at best sloppy. Many had to be returned to dealers for extra work. And, there was a big shortage of the ever-popular Chiefs.

Even with great models, Indian kept slipping farther and farther behind Harley-Davidson. In 1928, Indian produced 6,300 cycles to Harley's 22,350, preferring to experiment with electric refrigerators and automobile ventilators. One of two versions of the 1928 Indian catalog, featuring all models including the Indian Ace. ($100-300) *Courtesy of Bob "Sprocket" Eckardt.*

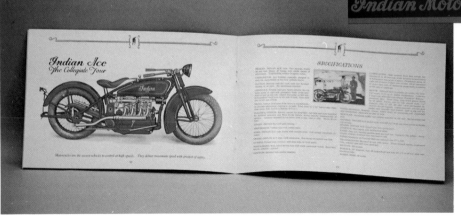

Indian Motocycle catalog, 1928, featuring twenty color pages of models including Collegiate Ace Four, Scout, Prince, Big Chief, Big Chief and Princess Sidecar, Service Car, Etc, 9" x 6". ($100-300) *Courtesy of the Dunbar Moonlight Kid Collection.*

Unfolded, this 1928 brochure has a blowup of the Scout 45 with new features. With a new 101 frame and a "Police Special" "45" motor, the Scout 45 is considered to be one of Indian's greatest designs. 17" x 18". ($50-125) *Courtesy of the Dunbar Moonlight Kid Collection.*

Here's another brochure that applauds the adventure of owning an Indian. While Indian should have been enjoying a bigger piece of the two-wheeled pie, too many Indian executives were plundering plums, which nearly forced Indian out of business. Indian Scout "New 101" and Indian 4 "New 402" fold-out brochure and poster with travel vignettes, includes mailer, 1929, 36" x 18". (Scarce, $75-250) *Courtesy of Dunbar Moonlight Kid Auctions.*

Indian fights the auto industry, promoting economical delivery, speed in traffic, and ease in parking. Unfortunately, the 101 Scout was dropped from the 1932 line as too expensive to build. Indian Scout Service Car fold-out brochure, 1928, photos of new vehicles and vehicles in use, 11" x 15 1/2". ($50-150) *Courtesy of the Dunbar Moonlight Kid Collection.*

The Indian 4 made its debut in 1929 with a brand new frame and front fork. Indian 4 Series 401 handbill announcement, circa 1929, 11" x 9". ($50-150) *Courtesy of the Dunbar Moonlight Kid Collection.*

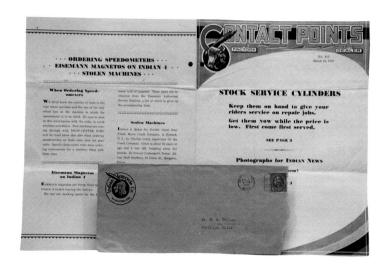

In a 1930 letter to factory dealers, with mailing envelope, Indian solicits parts orders, gives information, and asks for photos for the *Indian News.* 8 1/2" x 11". ($25-75) *Courtesy of the Dunbar Moonlight Kid Collection.*

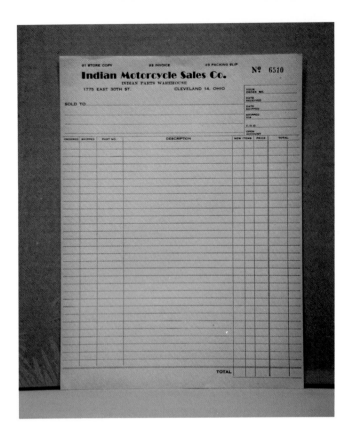

Indian Motocycle sales company order sheet, 1930s, 8" x 11". ($10-30) *Courtesy of the Dunbar Moonlight Kid Collection.*

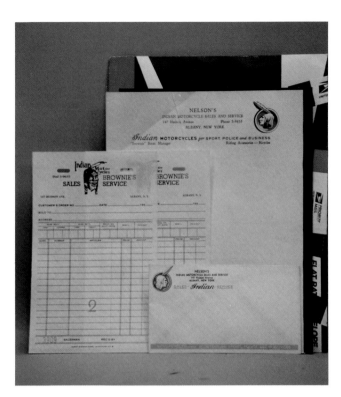

Four-piece stationery sets including two invoices for Brownie's Indian Motocycles, letterhead and an envelope for Nelson's Indian Motocycles. All show the same address and phone number, but there's a laughing Indian on Brownie's, a solemn Indian on Nelson's. ($30-100 for the lot) *Courtesy of Dunbar Moonlight Kid Auctions.*

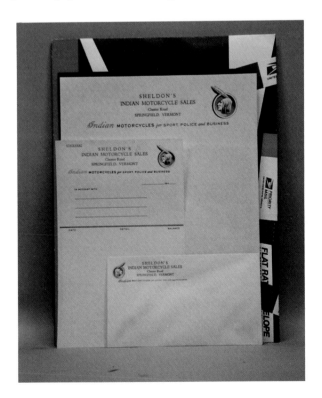

The early 1930s were nightmare years for Indian, as the company tried to recoup losses from former management's bad desicions, exploding flywheels and crankshafts in the Chief models, and an increasingly disenchanted network of dealers. Letter, statement forms, and small envelope, with Indian logo, from Sheldon's Indian Motocycle Sales, circa 1930s. ($20-75 Lot) *Courtesy of Dunbar Moonlight Kid Auctions.*

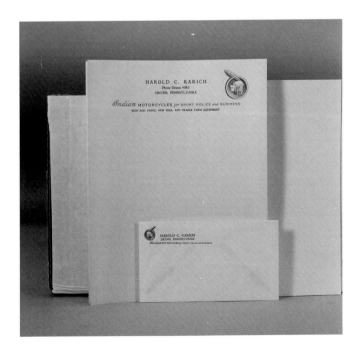

Indian Motocycles stationery and envelope set, Harold C. Rarich, Drums, Pennsylvania, with Indian logo, circa 1930s. ($20-75 for the set) *Courtesy of the Dunbar Moonlight Kid Collection.*

The 1930s were a time of reorganization for Indian. Motorcycle enthusiast E. Paul DuPont, of the DuPont paint and chemical family, took over the company in 1930. He spent the next decade trying to reignite the Indian magic, with mixed results. *Indian Commercial Motorcycles* sales booklet, 1936, 15 pages, chassis schematics, photo of commercially lettered cycle in actual use, includes dispatch tow, side van body and traffic car models, 8 1/2" x 5 1/2". ($50-150) *Courtesy of Dunbar Moonlight Kid Auctions.*

In the late 1930s, Indian created some of the most beautiful motorcycles ever built. Streamlined fenders were first offered in 1934–5 on the Chief and Sport Scout models, and customers could choose from the DuPont rainbow of colors for their bikes. Indian sales catalog, cover with factory entrance sign, 1938, 9" x 6". ($50-150) *Courtesy of Dunbar Moonlight Kid Auctions.*

In 1950, Ralph Rogers resigned. The company was taken over by an English concern. In 1953, the last year Indian produced an American motorcycle, the Springfield, Massachusetts, police force placed their first motorcycle order with Harley-Davidson, ending three decades of hometown Indian patronage. A year later, the Massachusetts State Police followed suit. Indian dealers now offered British Royal Enfields.

Sales literature from this era is varied, with many different models, showing scenes of happy bikers on the ten- nis courts, following Rogers' campaign to woo the middle class. As this was not the golden era of Indian, but the final bitter days, and because the quality of the literature (like the product line) wasn't that great, surviving memorabilia is not as desirable or valuable. It has its place in Indian history, so that may change in time. But, later Indian literature and posters will never hold the value or appeal of the early golden red era.

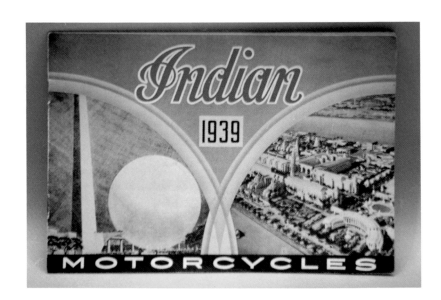

In honor of the 1939 New York World's Fair, Indian offered cycles in the fair's color scheme. This 1939 Indian booklet introduced new models including the Indian 4 Cylinder. Indian offered four-speed transmissions on the Chief and Indian 4. The line was beautiful— unfortunately engineering problems with the Chief and the upside-down valve Indian 4 helped to keep Indian from overtaking rival Harley-Davidson. 23 pages. ($50-175) *Courtesy of the Dunbar Moonlight Kid Collection.*

The year 1940 was a great one for Indian—the first year of the full flare-skirted fender. Sales almost equaled Harley's, with a profit of $700,000. Unfortunately, these successes would give away to World War II and new management. Indian color catalog with center fold-out "Spring Frame Motorcycles," sidecar on Model 440 Indian 4, and models 340, 440, 540, 640 solo bikes. Shows specifications and features. 1940, 14 pages, 9" x 6". ($50-125) *Courtesy of Bob "Sprocket" Eckardt.*

Paul DuPont sold his interests in Indian to Ralph Rogers in 1945. Rogers, a 36-year-old millionaire, wanted to offer Americans a line of lightweight cycles appealing to middle- and upper-class riders. Unfortunately, the vertical twin Scouts, Arrows, Warriors, and Braves never caught the public's imagination. Indian Arrow and Scout sales booklet, 1948, 22 pages of bikes and celebrities including Bob Feller, Vaughn Monroe, Ed Kretz, Jane Russell, Alan Ladd, Bobby Riggs, and features, 8" x 5". ($50-150) *Courtesy of Dunbar Moonlight Kid Auctions.*

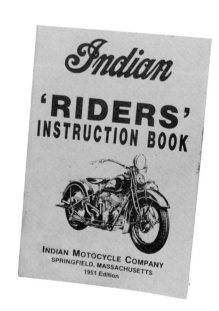

An attempt to bring customers into the tribe as early as possible, this Indian Papoose new folding portable motorcycle 97-pound "Pocket Prodigy" is detailed in a fold-out brochure with candid photos of the bike in use and specifications. Circa 1950, 4 pages, 5 1/2" x 8 1/2". ($30-85) *Courtesy of Dunbar Moonlight Kid Auctions.*

Indian Riders Instruction Book with fold-out lube chart, motorcycles, and Indian oil can, 1951, 42 pages, 5" x 7". ($25-75) *Courtesy of Barry and Arline MacNeil.*

Indian accessory catalogs are much rarer than their Harley counterparts. This factory publication shows clothing, jackets, goggles, "kidney" belts, hats, saddlebags, jewelry, parts, and accessories, and an oil can ad, making it a valuable reference tool. 1948, 8 1/2" x 11". ($50-150) *Courtesy of Bob "Sprocket" Eckardt.*

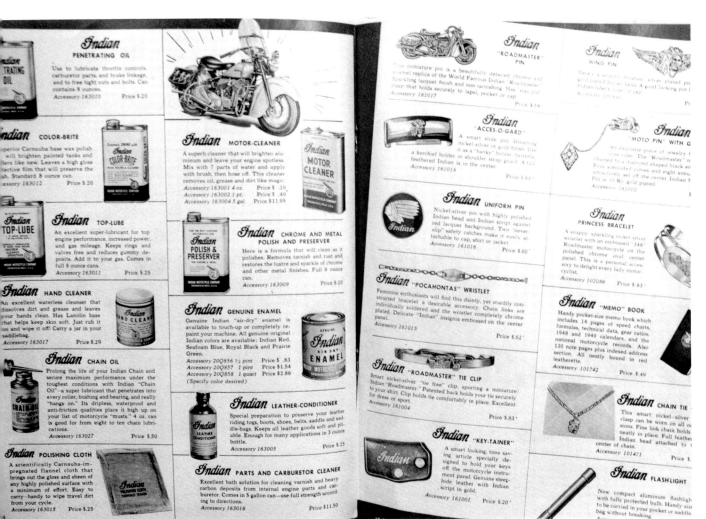

INDIAN'S NEW 10 STAR RACING SHIRT
SPECIALLY DESIGNED

*ZIPPER
CLOS

*RUGGED
ZIPP

*AIR VEN
ARM FI

*LIGHTWE
FASTEN
POC

*SMART FI
UNLIN

HEATHER YARN SHIRT (MAROON)
HEATHER YARN SHIRT (GRAY)

Short sleeve jersey pullover with Indian
design on left breast pocket. Smart appearance, light in weight. Fine quality combed
yarn, interlock cloth, smooth, soft firm
finish; washes beautifully, new style short
collar, rich velvety design.
SIZES: Small, Medium, Large.
Part #162140 (Maroon)   List $3.95
Part #162122 (Gray)   List $3.95

INDIAN SPORT SHIRT

Snowy white with sparkling red insignia
and trim on neck, sleeves and waist.
This washable cotton-rayon garment is
more popular than ever.
SIZES: Small, Medium, Large.
Part #950000   List $2.95

TWO-TONE RAYON JERSEY

Bright colors and smart tailoring make
this Indian rayon jersey outstanding.
Silver-grey body set off with brilliant
red sleeves and neck band, and red Indian
design. Extra full cut. Tucks inside
riding pants and stays put.
SIZES: Small, Medium, Large.
Part #102320   List $4.45

TURTLENECK JERSEY PULLOVER

This very new, very stylish jersey pullover has a zipper neck which can be worn
either turtleneck style or as an open
neckline with flat collar. The color is
silver-grey body, cardinal sleeves, neck,
and Indian script.
SIZES: Small, Medium, Large.
Part #162159   List $6.95

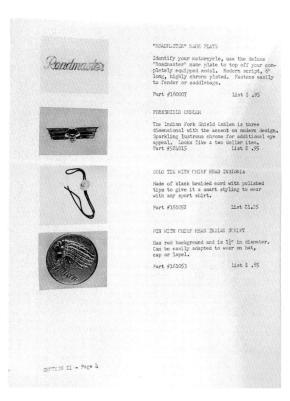

"ROADMASTER" NAME PLATE

Identify your motorcycle, use the deluxe
"Roadmaster" name plate to top off your completely equipped model. Modern script, 6"
long, highly chrome plated. Fastens easily
to fender or saddlebags.

Part #160007   List $ .95

FORESHIELD EMBLEM

The Indian Fork Shield Emblem is three
dimensional with the accent on modern design.
Sparkling lustrous chrome for additional eye
appeal. Looks like a two dollar item.
Part #524015   List $ .95

BOLO TIE WITH CHIEF HEAD INSIGNIA

Made of black braided cord with polished
tips to give it a smart styling to wear
with any sport shirt.

Part #161052   List $1.25

PIN WITH CHIEF HEAD INDIAN SCRIPT

Has red background and is 1¼" in diameter.
Can be easily adapted to wear on hat,
cap or lapel.

Part #161053   List $ .85

SECTION II - Page 4

This booklet shows just how far Indian had fallen since its halc
days, the items were probably old stock—the mystique was lon
gone. *Indian Accessories Catalog*, low-budget black and white
photos and descriptions of products, 1959 , 1959, 8 1/2" x 11".
(Scarce—$50-100) *Courtesy of the Dunbar Moonlight Kid Col
tion.*

100

Chapter 6

Chrome Ghosts
Miscellaneous Sales Literature and Paper

For those who only know two words about American motorcycling—Harley-Davidson—it must come as a shock to find out that between 1901–1916, New York state alone had more than thirty motorcycle manufacturers. It is estimated that during this era, 150-250 motorcycle companies or divisions were feeding the nation's newest hunger for freedom and adventure, without all that bothersome pedaling.

A number of the early motorcycle makers were already in business manufacturing other products, which helped to finance their new venture. Some, like bicycle manufacturers Schwinn, Pope, Columbia, Iver Johnson, Merkel, and Cleveland, had all been through the bicycle fad and probably figured this would be one way to stretch out the ride. Up until about 1910, most motorcycles were basically bicycles with clip-on drivetrains. At this point a new loop frame was developed, as was a V-twin motor. Motorcycles became a bit beefier and a were able to have more of their own character. Parts were integrated to fit the particular make.

The leader at this time, Indian, was generally far and away the best engineered and marketed motorcycle. Numerous racing victories and an extensive ad campaign help build the company into the largest motorcycle maker in the world.

In motorcycling's best year, 1913, 31,000 units were sold by Indian, 13,000 Harley-Davidson models, 11,000 Excelsiors, and then, surprisingly, 10,000 Flying Merkels, 6,500 Thors, and 5,000 Popes, with the rest of the sales spread out among the smaller companies. Two years later, eighty-five percent of American makers would cease production.

With a tremendous bicycle distribution organization in place, and a motorcycle known for comfort and performance, Pope could have been a stronger force. However, with the death of Colonel Pope in 1910, the guidance and managerial strength of the business was lost and the last year of production was 1914.

Likewise, Flying Merkel motorcycles were the brainchild of bicycle maker Joseph Merkel, who sold them through bicycle retailers. Flying Merkels were one of the few cycles, with Thor and Excelsior, that truly gave Indian a run for its feathers in dirt and board track racing. Like so many other companies, Merkels were forced to stop production in 1915 because of the difficulties in importing parts from Europe after fighting broke out.

Briggs & Stratton advertises its motor wheel bicycle attachment in a 16-page catalog, with illustrations of people, vehicles, and motorwheels in use, circa 1920, 8" x 10 1/2". (Rare—$100-300) *Courtesy of the Dunbar Moonlight Kid Collection.*

Excelsior had a great niche market, thanks to its fleet of well-built, four-cylinder cycles, added to later by Henderson. Police forces, in particular, loved the power and reliability offered by the X and Super X models. Ignatz Schwinn had the best dealer network setup, thanks to the extraordinary popularity of his Schwinn bicycles, and could outspend most other concerns. However, production dwindled consistently during the 1920s, and, at age 75, Schwinn was probably too tired to keep up the competition with Harley-Davidson and Indian and cope with The Depression. He shut down motorcycle production in March 1931.

If you read the ads in early trade publications, you'll notice that almost all of the ads, no matter how small the company, offer a catalog for those who request a copy. For those who love motorcycle history, these are the most sought-after pieces of literature about short-lived, long-forgotten makes. Depending on condition, graphics, and age, these catalogs should be worth between $100-$400 each. Of course, the dual-edged sword is that early and relatively unknown makers may not interest the vast majority of collectors, who may simply want a piece of Harley. But for those who do, they provide invaluable insight into the glory days of motorcycling.

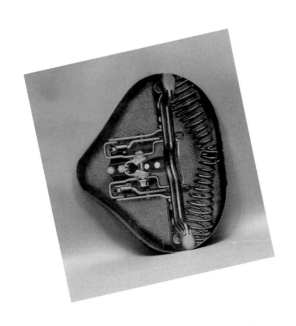

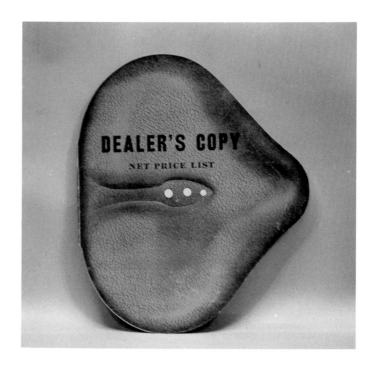

Testimonials from Cannonball Baker (who would know better about the characteristics of a motorcycle seat?) and other famous riders help give this George Masden Motorcycle Seat Catalog some distinction. 1917, 8 pages of photos and features, 8" x 9", (Rare—$100-300) *Courtesy of the Dunbar Moonlight Kid Collection.*

Bosch was the leader in providing magnetos to all forms of transportation and was particularly involved in racing. Bosch Magneto booklet for two-cylinder motorcycles with schematics and diagrams of Bosch ignition, circa 1915, 12 pages, 5 3/4" x 8 1/2". ($50-150) *Courtesy of the Dunbar Moonlight Kid Collection.*

The Bosch News, June 1910, an early, rare, and special publication detailing Bosch Magnetos contributions to the automotive racing, boating, motorcycling, and aeronautical worlds, with many photos including a New York motorcycle race meet with Indian bikes, MM, Reading-Standard, Crown, Flying Merker, and Yale, as well as Glenn Curtiss and Wright Aeroplane and Barney Oldfield. ($50-100) *Courtesy of the Dunbar Moonlight Kid Collection.*

Sometimes the accessory business was more lucrative than the actual motorcycle manufacturing business. Gotham Sporting Goods Co. catalog with accessories from Rogers sidecars, tires, goggles, tools, clothing, parts, etc., 1921, 70 pages, 6" x 9". ($50-125) *Courtesy of the Dunbar Moonlight Kid Collection.*

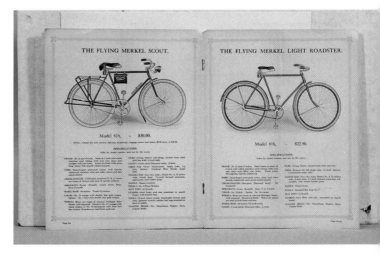

After seven years of moderate racing success and three years of sales exceeding 10,000 units a year, Miami Cycle Company was forced to close down its motorcycle division, in part because German-made ball bearings for engine components, for which Merkel was well known, were not available. Always a strong seller, Merkel returned to pedal power in 1916. Flying Merkel Bicycle Brochure with well-illustrated sketches of many models, component parts, and factory, 1916, 11 pages, 7 1/2" x 9" open. ($50-150) *Courtesy of the Dunbar Moonlight Kid Collection.*

Iver Johnson was a versatile man, first manufacturing firearms and then branching out into bicycles. In 1907, he came out with single-cylinder motorcycles. In 1912, Johnson first produced a heavyweight V-twin cycle. Iver Johnson hard-cover catalog featuring bicycles, a motorcycle, and a "Hammer the Hammer" handgun, great schematics, and detailed art work, 1912, 50 pages, 4 1/2" x 7". ($100-400) *Courtesy of the Dunbar Moonlight Kid Collection.*

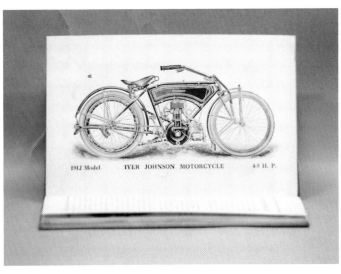

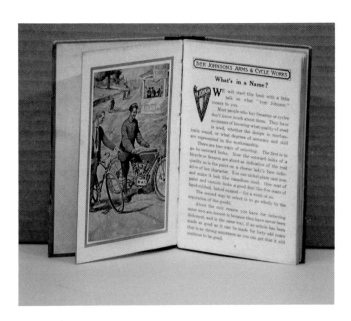

Great illustrations show the motorcycle at play in this Iver Johnson *Bicycles, Motorcycles, Firearms* hardcover book. 1915, 83 pages, 4 1/4" x 6 3/4". ($100-300) *Courtesy of the Dunbar Moonlight Kid Collection.*

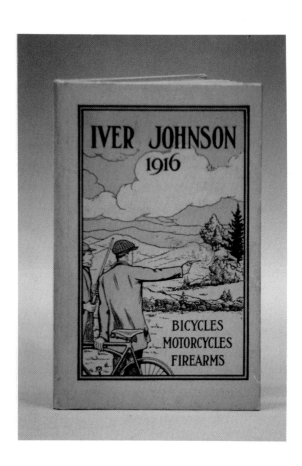

Iver Johnson discontinued its motorcycles in 1917, but still managed to produce their V-twins via special order until 1924. Known as rugged and dependable, these cycles were preferred by mail carriers. Iver Johnson Bicycles booklet with a variety of people on bicycles, well illustrated with photos and sketches of many models, 1917, 40 pages, 4 1/2" x 6 1/2". ($50-150) *Courtesy of the Dunbar Moonlight Kid Collection.*

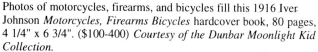

Photos of motorcycles, firearms, and bicycles fill this 1916 Iver Johnson *Motorcycles, Firearms Bicycles* hardcover book, 80 pages, 4 1/4" x 6 3/4". ($100-400) *Courtesy of the Dunbar Moonlight Kid Collection.*

Like many manufacturers, Yale was a bicycle name first. Later a single-cylinder motor was installed and another motorcycle came on the market during the explosion of makers in the early 1900s. Yale developed its own V-twin, which sold for $260. Like other makers, its parent company, Consolidated, took on munitions work during World War I and Yale sales faltered. In 1915, the line was finished. Yale Motorcycle Stationery, Consolidated Manufacturing Company, Toledo, Ohio, circa 1914, 8 1/2" x 11". ($20-75) *Courtesy of Dunbar Moonlight Kid Auctions.*

Ace was the brainchild of engineer William Henderson, who created the four-cylinder cycle after leaving Excelsior, the company to which he sold his Henderson four-cylinder rights. In 1922, Cannonball Baker took an Ace for a cross-country spin, his last transcontinental route, setting a new cross-country record of 6 days, 22 hours and 52 minutes. Unfortunately, Ace's euphoria was short lived as Henderson was killed soon after while test riding one of his cycles. Employees tried to keep the company afloat for several years, before finally selling out to Indian in 1927. Ace Motorcycles booklet and catalog with a feature on Ace's first fifteen years. 1926, 16 pages, 4" x 6". (Rare—$50-200) *Courtesy of Dunbar Moonlight Kid Auctions.*

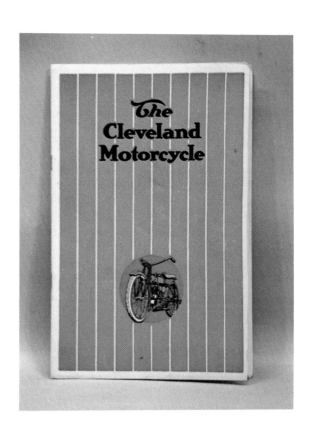

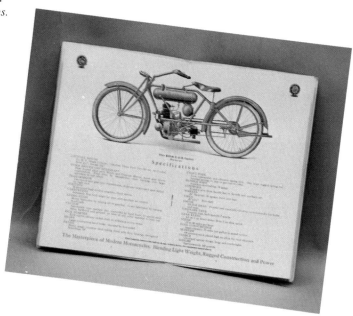

Cleveland, which built Cleveland and Chandler autos, was a rare maker in that the company actually started manufacturing utility motorcycles in 1915, when others were shutting down operations. In 1926, the company added a lightweight four-cylinder cycle, which never sold as well because by this time Indian and Harley refused to let their dealers carry other brands. In 1929, the company suspended production. Cleveland Motorcycle Catalog with centerfold of two-stroke model, 1919, 16 pages. (Rare—$100-350) *Courtesy of the Dunbar Moonlight Kid Collection.*

Evans Motorcycle fold-out sales brochure shows best features of the short-lived Powercycle from Cycle Motor Corporation, Rochester, New York. After 1921, the company went into very limited production and the manufacturing rights were sold to a German outfit. 1921, 13" x 12"open. ($15-75) *Courtesy of the Dunbar Moonlight Kid Collection.*

The Chicago-based Schwinn company of bicycle fame began producing the Excelsior line in 1907. In just a few years, Excelsior became one of the "Big Three," joining Harley and Indian in major market shares. By 1911, the Excelsior intake over exhaust valve twin, ridden by Joe Wolters, was beating Indian's superstar Jake DeRosier and making a run at Indian's racing dominance. Exceedingly rare 1910–12 Excelsior Auto Cycle catalog, 52 pages graphically illustrated with new model single-cylinder auto cycle, clothing, parts, and accessories. ($100-400) *Courtesy of Dunbar Moonlight Kid Auctions.*

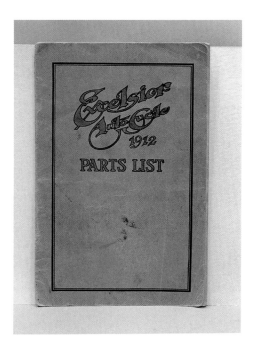

Financed by the Schwinn bicycle empire, Excelsior enjoyed the luxury of extensive advertising in trade publications. Its racing successes forced Oscar Hedstrom to design an eight-valve Indian to compete. 1912 Excelsior Auto Cycle Parts Catalog Serving 1908–12, 32 pages, illustrated. ($100-200) *Courtesy of Dunbar Moonlight Kid Auctions.*

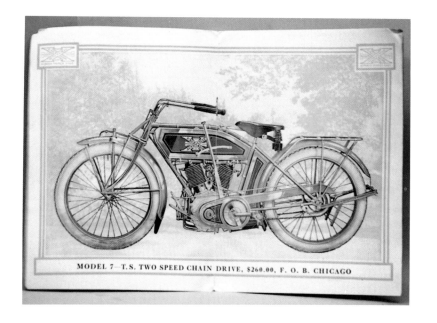

Excelsior 32-page Auto-Cycle color sales catalog, 1914, from Foster & Madsen, dealers out of Evan, Minnesota, featuring seven models including singles and twins and racing champions: Bob Perry, Carl Coldy, and Lee Humiston, holder of six world speed records including first motorcycle to officially break the 100-mile-per-hour barrier. This is also the year Joe Wolters won the Federation of American Motocyclists championship in Birmingham, Alabama. (Rare—$100-350) *Courtesy of Bob "Sprocket" Eckardt.*

This 1917 Excelsior Auto-Cycle catalog is a great introduction to the Excelsior world, from its factory and leader Ignaz Schwinn to the men who ran sales, shipping, etc. The centerfold pictures the "latest models." This was the year that Schwinn bought the Henderson motorcycle manufacturing rights in an attempt to move up from third in the "Big Three" pecking order. 32 pages. (Rare—$100-400) *Courtesy of Dunbar Moonlight Kid Auctions.*

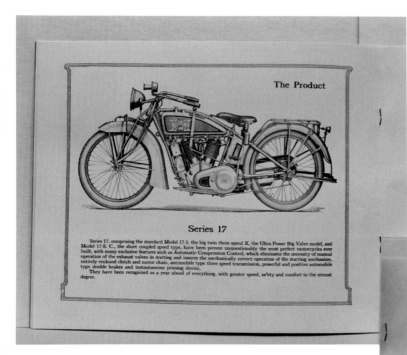

Excelsior, though producing less than Harley and Indian, managed to hang in during the 1920s thanks to profits from Schwinn's bicycling empire. Lack of dealer representation, The Depression, mechanical problems with the K models, and Schwinn's advancing age, all led to his decision to suspend operation of Excelsior and Henderson motorcycles on March 31, 1931. Early 1920s Excelsior Twin sales catalog, illustrated 12-page fold-out describes the new Excelsior system, centerfold of six new models, illustrated with schematics throughout. ($100-400) *Courtesy of Dunbar Moonlight Kid Auctions.*

111

Schwinn loved the Henderson 4-cylinder design and had a grip on the market until Indian bought out Ace in 1927. Early 1920s Henderson 4-cylinder sales catalog, 12-page fold-out with discourse on latest Henderson features, outstanding centerfold of six new models, and illustrated with schematics throughout. ($75-200) *Courtesy of Dunbar Moonlight Kid Auctions.*

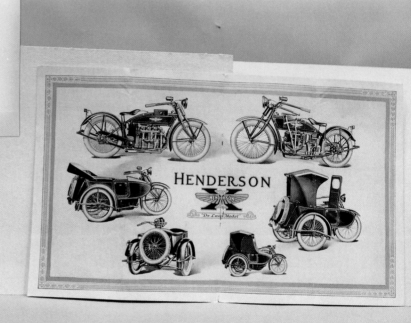

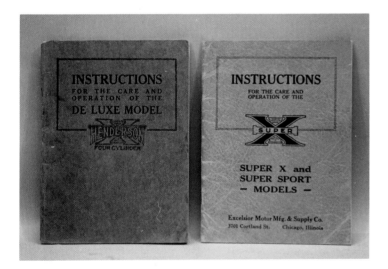

Excelsior instruction book for Super, Super X, and Super Sport models with diagrams showing full bike both sides & schematics of engine, etc, circa 1921, 32 pages, 5" x 6 1/2". ($50-150 each) *Courtesy of Dunbar Moonlight Kid Auctions.*

Tralette Motorcycle Trailer fold-out sales brochure, circa 1930s, 18" x 12" open. ($20-40) *Courtesy of the Dunbar Moonlight Kid Collection.*

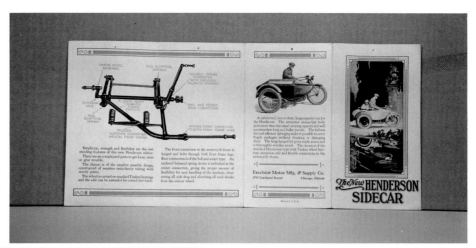

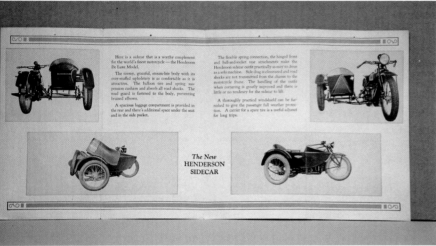

Henderson fold-out handbill featuring the new Henderson Sidecar, excellent photos and artwork. ($30-100) *Courtesy of the Dunbar Moonlight Kid Collection.*

General Motorcycle tires fold-out sales brochure, photos of Harleys, 1938, 18" x 12" open. ($20-50) *Courtesy of the Dunbar Moonlight Kid Collection.*

Chapter 7

A Shared History

Women in Motorcycling

Adeline and Augusta Van Buren, Clara Wagner, Dot Robinson, Vivian Bales, Gene Tierney, Linda Allen Dugeau, Bessie B. Stringfield, Vera Griffin, Helen Kiss Main, Linda Jackson, Cathy West, Cris Sommer, Becky Brown, Raquel Welch, Fran Crane, Mary Hart, Tami Rice, Jo Giovannoni, Kersten Hopkins, and, maybe, you

What's the question to this answer? Give a human timeline to women's motorcycling. All of the above have contributed to the history, culture, sport and/or promotion of women's cycling. These contributions might barely blip on the testosterone chart right now. However, thanks to a biker babe boom of the 1980s-90s, close to a million women are following the former trailblazers' lead.

Women have ridden motorcycles just as long as men have, only in smaller numbers and with less media coverage. So their exploits, like those of their fellow female pilots, have been viewed more as oddities (and occasional threats) than as equal accomplishments.

Because fewer women have ridden cycles and because documentation in many instances has not been extensive, any memorabilia associated with women's cycling is desirable and difficult to accrue. Occasionally, you can run across some postcards with anonymous women riders. Harley-Davidson, of course, recognized women as potential customers early on and often ran articles in *The Enthusiast* about women riders (usually with their husbands) and promoted clothing specifically made for women.

In 1910, eighteen-year-old Clara Wagner, whose father was one of the earliest motorcycle manufacturers, rode in a 365-mile endurance race, from Chicago to Indianapolis, achieving a perfect score and beating most of the men. However, the Federation of American Motorcyclists refused to acknowledge her victory. You can find Clara on a trade postcard advertising the short-lived Wagner motorcycle.

On July 4, 1916, sisters Adeline and Augusta Van Buren (descendants of former president Martin Van Buren) declared their independence by hopping on a pair of brand new Indian Powerplus cycles and, in the best Cannonball Baker tradition, taking off from New York for California. Keep in mind that in 1916 the automobile was still a novelty, so the nation's road system was uneven at best, with little to no pavement. This fact did not deter the duo. On

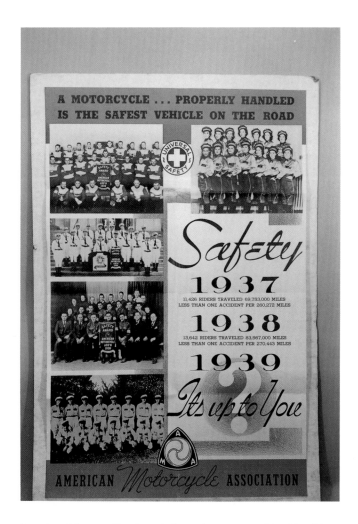

American Motorcyclist Association safety poster, 1937–39, with club photos including one of fifteen women riders. Individual clubs were the precursor to the Motor Maids, 25" x 38". ($50-150) *Courtesy of the Dunbar Moonlight Kid Collection.*

their way out West, they became the first women to climb the 14,000 feet to the top of Pike's Peak in Colorado. The Van Burens arrived in California sixty days later, proving they were more than capable for their subsequent work as dispatch riders for the military.

Fast forward to the 1930s, the beginning of the Dot Robinson era. Aviation had Amelia Earhart. Women's motorcycling has been fortunate to have Dot Robinson as the sport's Jackie Robinson. Dot's family, the Gouldings, came over from Australia as her father, James, was a sidecar builder who wanted to break into the American market. Born in 1912, Dot learned to ride when she was knee high to a V-twin, married fellow motorcycle enthusiast Earl Robinson at age nineteen, and soon after bought out her father's Harley dealership, moving it to Detroit.

With the first motorized bicycles of the early–1900s, women were just as fascinated by the freedom that motorcycles offered as their male counterparts. In 1910, 18-year old Clara Wagner—whose father built the short-lived Wagner Motorcycles out of St. Paul, Minnesota—got a perfect score in a 365-mile endurance race from Chicago to Indianapolis. Many more female feats were to follow Photo postcard of two women on an early one-cylinder motorcycle, maker unknown. ($10-30) *Courtesy of the Dunbar Moonlight Kid Collection.*

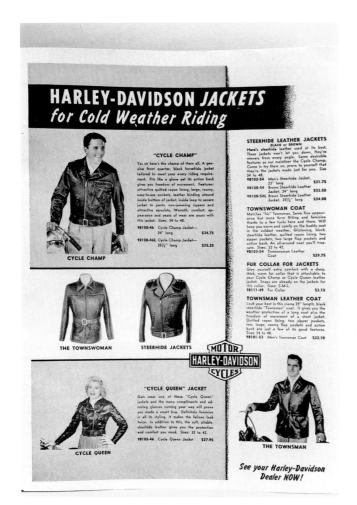

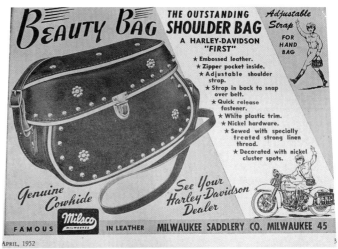

Harley-Davidson has proven itself remarkably pro-woman, willing to promote women's biking. Someone was astute enough to realize the marketing possibilities. Maybe longtime rider and Harley dealer Dot Robinson had some influence. Nonetheless, ads like this one from the April 1952 issue of American Motorcycling for the Harley "Beauty Bag," became particularly prevalent in the 1950s. *Courtesy of the Dunbar Moonlight Kid Collection.*

Whether they were relegated to sidecars or actually behind the throttle, motorcycle magazines and accessory catalogs often catered to women, especially Harley-Davidson which offered a variety of specially designed hats, jackets, etc., for women. Hey, who wouldn't want to be known as the "Cycle Queen" of their town? This ad is from the November 1953 issue of American Motorcycling. *Courtesy of the Dunbar Moonlight Kid Collection.*

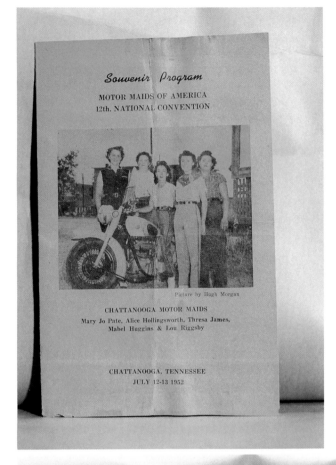

For neat and orderly hair (but no protection from spills) rider's caps were offered to women riders. This example, from the 1950s, is made of rayon with a chin strap. Harley made a similiar version called the "Cyclette." $50-125) *Courtesy of Bob "Sprocket" Eckardt.*

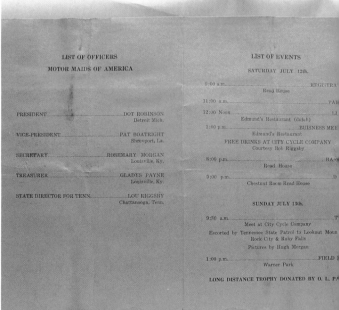

Motor Maids of America was founded by Dot Robinson and Linda Dugeau in 1940, after a three-year search to find fifty women who embodied the qualities Dot and Linda were looking for: neat and clean, upstanding citizens who loved to ride. The first convention took place in 1944—fourteen members attended. Motor Maids of America 1949 Convention Pennant, Union City, Tennessee, July 9–10. ($75-250) *Courtesy of the Dunbar Moonlight Kid Collection.*

The Motor Maids still hold their annual conventions every July, with roughly half of their 500-plus membership attending. Souvenir program from twelfth national Motor Maids convention, July 1952, Chattanooga ,Tennessee, listing officers and events, 5 1/2" x 8 1/2". ($10-40) *Courtesy of the Dunbar Moonlight Kid Collection.*

116

After receiving their American Motorcyclist Association charter in 1940, the The Motor Maids immediately adopted uniforms. In the 1950s, the official uniform became the trademark blue shirt, grey trousers, and white belt still worn to this day. Motormaids of America sweater, 1950s. ($50-100) *Courtesy of Bob"Sprocket" Eckardt.*

Shield-shaped Motor Maid Inc. decal, circa 1960, 3 1/2" x 3 1/2". ($5-15) *Courtesy of the Dunbar Moonlight Kid Collection.*

Grace Hall's Motor Maids uniform from the 1950s, with "Grace" embroidered on pocket, white tie, and "Motor Maids from Indiana" embroidered on back, with grey uniform trousers. ($50-150) *Courtesy of the Dunbar Moonlight Kid Collection.*

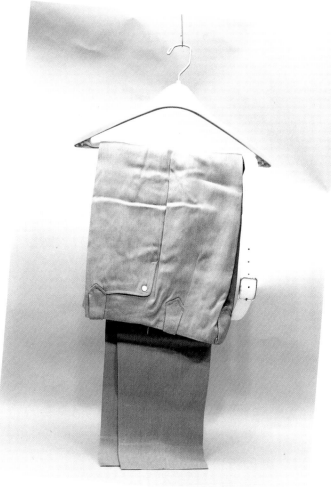

Uniforms were important for the image of the Motor Maids as women riders with solid values and morals. Shirt with "Motormaids from Admire, Kansas" on back, "Betty" over the pocket, Early–60s. ($50-100) *Courtesy of the Dunbar Moonlight Kid Collection.*

Motormaid naugahide clip-on tie has the motormaid shield, made of hard plastic with military tack, early–60s, this tie has been replaced with a cloth tie and may be a little less likely to fall off while passing through those mud patches. ($25-75) *Courtesy of the Dunbar Moonlight Kid Collection.*

By the 1950s, as an arm of the American Motorcycling Association, the Motor Maids were recognized to the point where they received their own monthly news column in the association's magazine, *American Motorcycling*. The American Motorcyclist Association realized that the more they helped to promote the Motor Maids, the more women would want to become members, a 90-degree change in attitude from the days when E. C. Smith was at the helm of the organization. *Courtesy of Dunbar Moonlight Kid Auctions.*

Dot Robinson, as founder and 25-year president, was always front and center in Motor Maids photos. And she deserved to be—she has logged more than 1.5 million miles on cycles and earned her title of "The First Lady of Motorcycling." American Motorcycling Magazine, November 1953, featuring Motor Maids of America at their annual convention. ($10-25) *Courtesy of Dunbar Moonlight Kid Auctions.*

Dot Robinson, class a sidecar winner of the 1940 Jack Pine Two-Day Endurance Run. The President of the American Motorcyclist Association, E. C. Smith, did not want women competing, but Dot petitioned the Competition Committee to accept her entries. With Dot's winning ways, and the fact that she had the ear of Arthur Davidson (she and husband Earl were persuaded by Arthur to be Harley dealers), E. C. Smith could do nothing. The sidecar, of course, is a Goulding, made by Dot's father, James. *Courtesy of Dunbar Moonlight Kid Auctions.*

A rare photo of Dot Robinson in black leather from the Ohio Tour of May 1949. Dot occasionally wore black until "that awful movie," as she called "The Wild Ones." After its release she never wore black leather again. She switched to pink and never looked back. ($10-30) *Courtesy of the Dunbar Moonlight Kid Collection.*

Women who defied convention pose at their own convention, with Dot Robinson standing to left of longtime member and friend Mabel Aston. *Courtesy of the Dunbar Moonlight Kid Collection.*

Dot Robinson and her Electra Glide make front-page news after logging a million miles. Dot is known for her pink Harleys, probably the inspiration for Mary Kay and her pink "make-up mobiles." In 1935, at the age of 23, Dot and husband, Earl, set a transcontinental sidecar record of 89 hours, 58 minutes. *American Motorcycling Magazine,* February 1968, 38 pages. ($10-30) *Courtesy of the Dunbar's Moonlight Kid Auctions.*

122

Photo of Motor Maid Mabel Aston on her Harley at Lockport, Ohio, May 1946. ($5-20) *Courtesy of the Dunbar Moonlight Kid Collection.*

Photo of Motor Maid Edna Renfrow on a Royal Enfield at a bike meet in Fort Wayne, Indiana in 1947. ($5-20) *Courtesy of the Dunbar Moonlight Kid Collection.*

Longtime Motor Maid Mabel Aston changes brands, seen here on her Indian in Parkersburg, West Virginia, while on the Ohio Tour, May 1949. Does she know something we don't? ($5-20) *Courtesy of the Dunbar Moonlight Kid Collection.*

Motor Maid Grace Hall takes a break from the open road at the entrance to Skyline Drive, July 1943. ($5-20) *Courtesy of the Dunbar Moonlight Kid Collection.*

Motor Maid Evelyn Hame poses between two bikes in Marion, Ohio, while on tour in May 1949. ($5-20) *Courtesy of the Dunbar Moonlight Kid Collection.*

Photo of Motor Maid Mary Wall astride a bike on Main Street, Parkersburg, West Virginia, May 1951. ($5-20) *Courtesy of the Dunbar Moonlight Kid Collection.*

Motor Maids photo taken during an Ohio Caverns Tour, May 21-22, 1949. Members pictured include Dot Robinson, front row, third from the left, and Grace Hall, second row, third from the right. At this point the maids hadn't adopted their trademark blue and grey uniforms. ($10-30) *Courtesy of the Dunbar Moonlight Kid Collection.*

Motor Maid Mabel H. Black and her daughters in Acton Indiana, September 1954. The women are posed with a Goulding Rocket sidecar bike and solo bikes. ($5-20) *Courtesy of the Dunbar Moonlight Kid Collection.*

In 1930, Dot won her first trophy in the Flint 100 Enduro men's sidecar class with a score of 1,000 points. She entered her first Jack Pine two-day, 500-mile endurance race in 1934, known as the most grueling challenge in motorcycle racing, but because her feet couldn't touch the ground, she entered in the sidecar division, on a Harley 74 with Goulding sidecar. Dot came in fourth in the sidecar class. Six years later, in 1940, she won her class, sending American Motorcycling Association President E. C. Smith into fits. During the 1930s, Dot placed or won in more than fifty endurance runs. Harley even put Dot one of its 1940 posters, along with solo winner Ted Konecny.

Dot didn't stop there. In 1941, she founded the country's first national women's motorcycling organization, the Motor Maids, with friend Linda Dugeau, after spending three years searching for fifty women who met their standards of character, citizenship, and appearance. And, of course, they had to be able to ride. Fifty-six years later, the Motor Maids still hold annual conventions and promote fellowship (or gal-ship?) via motorcycling. Both men and women love to collect Motor Maids memorabilia, including programs, pennants, ribbons, uniforms, trophies, and photos.

Dot raced until 1971, retiring to Florida where she still rides her pink Harley at age 84. She is truly the first lady of motorcycling, with more than a million and a half miles behind her and who knows how many still ahead of her. Her collection of trophies and memorabilia is priceless, a tribute to her determination and love of the sport.

Numerous women have taken Dot's lead in organizing and informing women on bikes. Longtime riders Cris Sommer and Jo Giovannoni started the magazine Harley Women, dedicated to informing women motorcyclists about each other. Harley sprang an offshoot of its Harley Owner Groups (HOGS) called Ladies on Harleys. In 1979, Becky Brown of Ohio started a club called Women in the Wind, which now has more than 600 members in the United States, Canada, England, and New Zealand. In 1982, Women on Wheels was founded by Arleen Ruby. With a membership of 1,800 women in the United States and Canada, it is the largest women's motorcycling club.

Celebrities have also helped promote the image that biking is cool for women as well as men. In the 1940s, actress Gene Tierney rode a Harley. In the 1960s, Raquel Welch liked to relax on her Triumph, once she could get it kick started. Today it's not unusual to see singers k. d. lang, Tanya Tucker, or Wynonna Judd straddling the saddle, or even a more mainstream personality like Mary Hart talking about her latest two-wheeled trip. Liz Taylor made magazine covers (again) in the late 1980s when Malcolm Forbes bought her a custom-made purple Harley Sportster named Passion, after her first fragrance. Even Texas Governor Ann Richards took on a new challenge at 60, getting herself a Harley for her birthday.

Thanks to Dot Robinson's pioneering, hundreds of women are racing, from Fran Crane's endurance runs and sprints to Linda Jackson's drag racing exploits to Kathleen Coburn on super bikes to Kersten Hopkins who, at the age of 16 in 1995, became the youngest nitro pilot ever.

What's next? Maybe a movie that actually portrays a woman on a motorcycle as a woman and not as some sprocketing sex toy or man hater? Stay tuned.

Women's motorcycle memorabilia has extra value in that it may add a piece to the history puzzle that was not known previously, a puzzle that still has a long way to go before the whole picture is complete.

In full uniform, Motor Maids pose in Columbus Ohio. Dot Robinson is on the far right, first row. Circa 1950s. ($10-30) *Courtesy of the Dunbar Moonlight Kid Collection.*

Motor Maids mug for the camera, probably after a tour. Dot Robinson and Mabel Aston are front and center. Circa 1950. ($10-30) *Courtesy of the Dunbar Moonlight Kid Collection.*

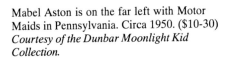

Mabel Aston is on the far left with Motor Maids in Pennsylvania. Circa 1950. ($10-30) *Courtesy of the Dunbar Moonlight Kid Collection.*

Motor Maids stand before the nation's capitol in Washington, D.C., Dot and Mabel in the front row. Circa 1950s. ($10-30) *Courtesy of the Dunbar Moonlight Kid Collection.*

The Motor Maids in Peoria pose outdoors with their bikes behind them. Circa 1950s. ($10-30) *Courtesy of the Dunbar Moonlight Kid Collection.*

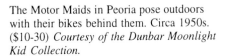

At the 1947 National Motor Maid Convention, Dot Robinson, Vera Griffin, and Helen Kiss Main pose on three bikes. Notice that these were pre-helmet days. Vera Griffin, from Columbus, Indiana, a toolmaker, logged more than a million miles on her Harleys and Triumphs over sixty years. Helen Kiss Main, of Pottstown, Pennsylvania, was the Motor Maids' first treasurer. She liked to outdo Dot with her own pink Indian and matching outfits. ($15-40) *Courtesy of the Dunbar Moonlight Kid Collection.*

Three Motor Maids hold their trophies, from left, unknown, Dot Robinson, and Ilene Tilson of Missouri. In 1930, Dot won her first trophy in the Flint 100 Enduro men's sidecar class with a score of a thousand points. During the 1930s alone, competing exclusively against men, Dot won or placed in more than fifty endurance runs. Circa 1950s. ($15-40) *Courtesy of the Dunbar Moonlight Kid Collection.*

Helen Chaney poses on a fully dressed Indian in Columbus, Indiana, in 1949. ($5-20) *Courtesy of the Dunbar Moonlight Kid Collection.*

The Motor Maids at a Cumberland, Maryland, race banquet in 1953. The group includes Dot Robinson and Mabel Aston, with other members' names and addresses written on the back. Dot raced for forty years, retiring in 1971. ($10-30) *Courtesy of the Dunbar Moonlight Kid Collection.*

In Cumberland, Maryland, Dot Robinson awards a second-place trophy to Donna Lou Miller, Mabel Aston gives winner Joan Youngson her trophy and a long-distance award is given to Ilene Tilson of Princeton, Missouri by Marge Hartman in 1953. ($10-30) *Courtesy of the Dunbar Moonlight Kid Collection.*

More than a hundred Motor Maids pose in full uniform at a meeting in Painsville, Ohio, in 1975, including Dot Robinson. ($10-30) *Courtesy of the Dunbar Moonlight Kid Collection.*

128

Chapter 8

Motorcycling on Screen
Film Posters: A Triumph in Print

David Gaylin is the owner of Motor Cycle Days, a business that buys and sells both foreign and domestic motorcycle paper and posters. David takes his mobile gallery and book stall to just under thirty antique motorcycle rallies in the eastern United States and has also built a thriving mail order business.

Living in Baltimore, Maryland, exposed him to a major distributor of Triumph motorcycles. He says that he "found the compact size and poetic lines of Triumphs more attractive to a 5-foot, 4-inch art student than the massive (and agricultural) Milwaukee V-twins. Collecting sales brochures and related literature was also a part of the theme and many times I could be seen thieving catalogs (and anything else) in the Tricor lobby." David was in the right place at the right time to pick up a big haul when the distributor was closed down in 1975. This catch only led to a hunt for more Triumph material and culminated in a 224-page book, *Triumph Motorcycles in America*, co-written with Lindsay Brooke.

While researching his book in 1991, David met the late Clyde Earl, a retired United States Triumph employee and walking encyclopedia on motion picture history and, in particular, motorcycles in film. Clyde lived within a stone's throw of all the major Hollywood studios and had an intimate relationship with many who worked in the film industry, including many well-known motorcycle stuntmen. Through this relationship, David received his education in motorcycle movie art and also established a rich source of contacts. To date he has collected or recorded more than five hundred examples of motorcycle movie art and images, beginning with the silent film era. For David, motorcycle movies and their advertisements continue to be a passion.

The following photos and text are courtesy of David Gaylin, Motor Cycle Days:

Film Posters: A Triumph in Print
David Gaylin

Because of their vivid colors and often eye-popping artwork, original movie advertising posters have long been sought by collectors and those wanting to energize showrooms and restaurant decor. Frequently artistic, these prints were originally created for theatre lobbies (or external showcases) and used as a vehicle to invite ticket sales. These posters should not be confused with personality prints, which are usually enlarged images of a celebrity created for the purpose of publicity or the exploitation thereof. These, too, can achieve elevated values and will be examined later.

As with all collectibles, a movie poster's value is diminished or enhanced, depending on its condition. These were promotional tools and, when originally displayed, little thought was given to their survival. So prints that have suffered from solar bleaching or that exhibit large water stains will not be worth the same as fresher examples. Holes (and their locations) will also spoil a poster's value, but creases from folding generally do not. In many cases, these posters have survived only because they were folded and most collectors accept the creases as part of the hobby. Folds can be eliminated or minimized by having the posters backed with linen.

By the 1940s, American movie advertising posters were standardized into roughly five different sizes (and formats).

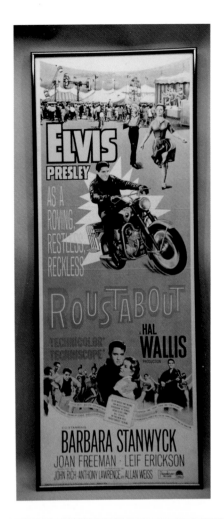

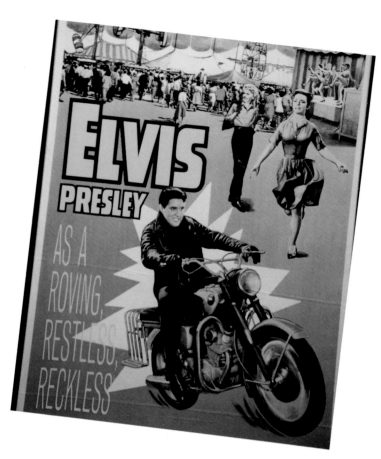

Elvis Presley lobby card plugs *Roustabout* with graphics of the "roving, restless, and reckless" young man tearing through the fair on his bike, 1964, 14" x 36", framed. ($100-250) *Courtesy of Dunbar Moonlight Kid Auctions.*

Easy Rider one sheet (Style C), 1969. ($100-250) *Courtesy of David Gaylin—Motorcycle Days.*

Angels Hard as They Come, one sheet. ($50-100) *Courtesy of David Gaylin—Motorcycle Days.*

Hell's Angels '69, one sheet, 1969. ($50-100) *Courtesy of David Gaylin—Motorcycle Days.*

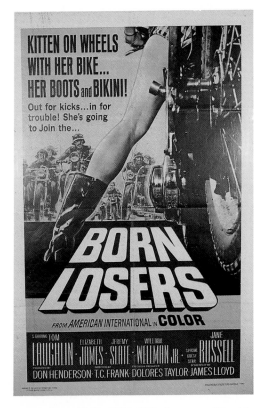

Born Losers, one sheet, 1967. ($100-150) *Courtesy of David Gaylin—Motorcycle Days.*

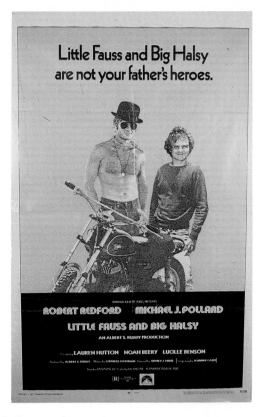

Little Fauss and Big Halsy, one sheet, 1970. ($50-100) *Courtesy of David Gaylin—Motorcycle Days,*

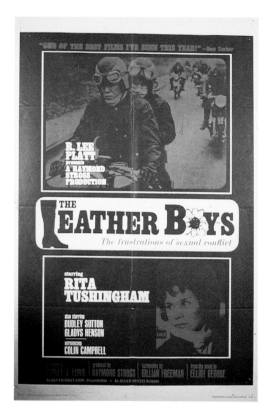

Leather Boys, one sheet, rare cult classic from 1966. ($75-100) *Courtesy of David Gaylin—Motorcycle Days.*

Werewolves on Wheel, one sheet, 1971. ($75-150) *Courtesy of David Gaylin—Motorcycle Days.*

The Pace That Thrills, one sheet, 1952. ($100-175) *Courtesy of David Gaylin—Motorcycle Days.*

Electraglide in Blue, one sheet, (style B), 1973. ($50-75) *Courtesy of David Gaylin—Motorcycle Days.*

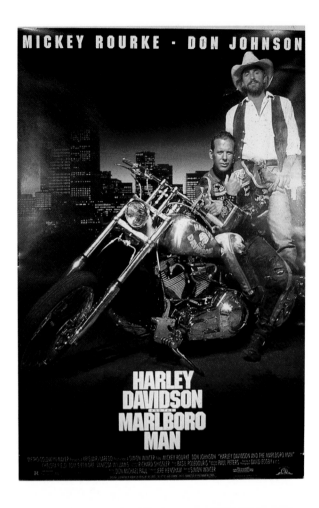

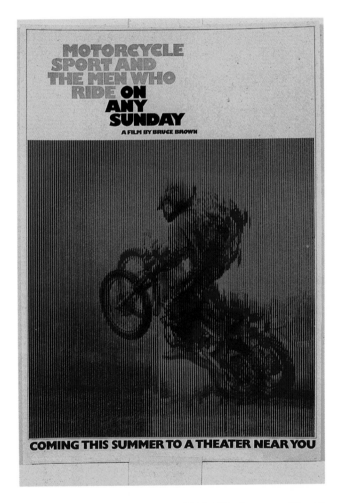

Harley-Davidson and the Marlboro Man, one sheet. ($25-50)
Courtesy of David Gaylin—Motorcycle Days.

On Any Sunday, one sheet, 1970. ($100-200) *Courtesy of David Gaylin—Motorcycle Days.*

Mannequin, one sheet. ($25-40) *Courtesy of David Gaylin—Motorcycle Days.*

One-sheets are the most common poster and *usually* the most desirable. They measure twenty-seven by forty-one inches tall, with the artwork displayed vertically. Until the mid-1980s, these were sent to theatres folded, after which time folded one-sheets became available. The original art is usually laid out in this format and then rearranged for the other sizes. However, there may be several different one-sheets depending on how ambitious (i.e., expensive) the advertising campaign. Different styles are denoted by letter (A through D) and found on the border at the bottom.

The year can be determined by the National Screen Service marking at the bottom edge that was printed on all movie material until recently. The two-part number first indicates the year of release, while the second figure assigns the film's numerical order of production within the year. On folded posters, this number and the film's title were stamped on one of the outer surfaces to obviate unnecessary unfolding.

One-sheets should not be confused with video store posters which are slightly smaller in dimension and usually found in rolled condition. Video posters are most associated with releases from the 1980s and later, but several motorcycle prints have already attained appreciable value, such as *Hell's Angels Forever* ($50-$150) and *The Wild Ones* ($50-$150), which features a close-up of (a much younger and thinner) Marlon Brando, his trophy, and his Triumph.

Half-sheets, as their name implies, are roughly half of a one-sheet poster and measure twenty-two by twenty-eight inches tall. Similar or rearranged one-sheet graphics are used, but in a horizontal layout and these can be found in either folded or rolled condition. They usually aren't as desirable as the larger print, but there are exceptions. Their smaller size renders them practical for use in the home.

Insert posters were created to fit narrower display cases and are again usually based on the one-sheet art. They measure fourteen by thirty-six inches tall and the image is viewed vertically. These were also sent to theatres folded or rolled in a tube. Inserts are attractive to those with a narrow wall space to fill, but they generally don't command the price of the larger posters.

Three-sheet posters are three times the size of a one-sheet with the image displayed vertically. They were printed in three sections of thinner paper and when assembled measure twenty-seven by eight-one inches tall. However, the larger size is often an encumbrance to collectors and it is not uncommon to see one-sheets carry more value. The same can also be said of the enormous billboard-size six-sheets and twenty-four-sheets.

Much smaller, **lobby cards** were created to show various scenes of a movie with the intent to stimulate viewer interest. Usually in sets of eight, each card carries a different photograph from the film printed on card stock. Before the 1980s, many lobby cards also incorporated elements of the one-sheet graphics in an enlarged border at the bottom and left side. Their handy size, fourteen by eleven inches tall, makes them easy to store or display. With matting the make super wall hangings. Their value depends largely on the movie as well as the image contained and can range anywhere from $5 to $25. However, scene cards showing the film's principals on motorcycles, such as in *Easy Rider, The Wild Ones,* and *The Great Escape* can trade for as much as $100.

Elvis Presley was motorcycle-mounted in at least four of his movies and any lobby card (or poster) showing him on a bike from *Roustabout, Clambake, Stay Away Joe,* or *Viva Las Vegas* has an elevated value.

Although not as common in the United States, **British quad posters** also deserve mention. These measure approximately thirty by forty inches tall and have horizontal graphics sometimes similar to the American one-sheets, other times with completely different art. Because of their wide format, they are generally not as desirable as the one-sheet posters. However, in a few cases such as with *The Wild Ones,* British quads have equal value to their American cousins (original 1953 release US one-sheets show only an image of Marlon, while UK posters have him on the bike— value of either; $150-$350).

In addition to all these, a movie was sometimes re-released after a few years with completely new artwork. As a rule, re-release posters aren't as desirable as the advertising issued for a first run. A case in point is *Born Losers,* where the original one-sheet ($100-$150) features a great worm's eye view of a bad girl on a bike. With the success of Tom Laughlin in *Billy Jack* in 1972, a sequel to B*orn Losers,* which was re-released with a poster prominently featuring Laughlin without any motorcycles ($25). Billy Jack was a character in the first movie.

However, there are exceptions to any rule. All three styles of the original *Easy Rider* one-sheets ($100-$250) show only a back view of a pensive Peter Fonda and no motorcycle, while the art found on the 1972 re-release posters contains an image of both Fonda and Dennis Hopper on their choppers ($150-$350), making these prints more desirable.

Some of the most highly valued artwork today are movie posters in the science fiction, horror, and exploitation genres. Certain posters advertising the films *Forbidden Planet, King Kong,* and *Dracula* are currently bringing six figures! Motorcycle movie art isn't in this league yet, but when there is a crossover into other genres, such as the outrageous *Werewolves on Wheels* ($75-$150) or *Psychomania* ($75-$150), values can be positively effected. Another example of this is one of the most sought-after, motorcycle-related prints today, the Russ Meyer camp classic *Motorpsycho* ($250-$500).

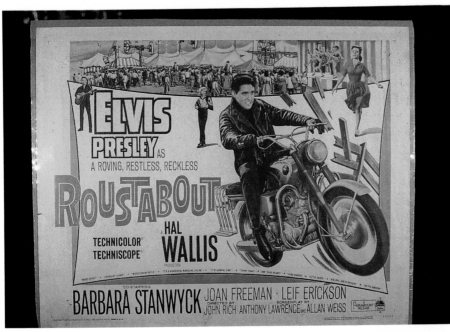

Roustabout, half sheet, 1964. ($100-400)
*Courtesy of David Gaylin—Motorcycle
Days.*

On Any Sunday, half sheet, 1970. ($75-150)
*Courtesy of David Gaylin—Motorcycle
Days.*

Easy Rider, lobby card pictures movie
principals Hopper, Fonda, and Nicholson on
bikes, 1969. ($25-100) *Courtesy of David
Gaylin—Motorcycle Days.*

The Great Escape, lobby card picturing
Steve McQueen on bike, 1963. ($25-50)
*Courtesy of David Gaylin—Motorcycle
Days.*

Drive-in movie posters of the '50s and '60s that feature motorcycles have become very desirable, in particular those in the "bad girl" or "juvenile" categories. Of these, *She-devils on Wheels* ($150-$350) leads the pack, so to speak, followed closely behind by *Miniskirt Mob* ($!00-$250), and *Hell's Belles* ($75-$150). *Dragstrip Riot* was a 1958 drive-in flick about hot rods, but the fantastic poster art depicts a couple in a Corvette being pursued by a gang of wrench-wielding motorcyclists. In this case, the half-sheet ($100-$250) is perhaps the most desirable to motorcycle collectors as its horizontal format allows the entire pack of Triumph riders to be seen. Other forgettable motorcycle movies from the 1950s that spawned great posters include *The Pace That Thrills* ($100-$175) and *Motorcycle Gang* ($100-$250), the latter in duo-tone showing the film's principals fist fighting while laying over a BSA Gold Star.

Black and white personality posters are the enlarged images of movie stars (i.e., James Dean, Marlon Brando, Marilyn Monroe) found on poster racks in gift shops, music stores, etc. They were not generally used to advertise a movie and usually contain no artwork. However, some of the older and out-of-print posters from the 1960s, such as those of Brigitte Bardot (and motorcycle) or Steve McQueen jumping the fence in *The Great Escape*, are difficult to find and often mandate a strong price ($50-$200), depending on condition.

With values of movie posters still appreciating, copies are bound to turn up and there is no easy way to tell a fake from an original if a proper job has been carried out. The best advice is to get to know the person or dealer who is offering it. Is he or she well known within the hobby? Will they stand behind (and make good on) what they sell? An honorable dealer will go out of his way to avoid even the slightest stain on their reputation. It's also a good idea to read everything on your topic and attend as many collector shows as possible.

AUTHOR'S NOTE: In running auctions and dealing in motorcycle collectibles for the past ten years, I've found this to be one of the most undervalued areas of the collectibles market, right after The Enthusiast *magazines. A number of music and movie stars have always been drawn to motorcycles, from Clark Gable and Van Johnson to Vaughn Monroe and, probably the most famous celebrity competitive rider, Steve McQueen. Today such stars as Jay Leno, Mary Hart, the Doobie Brothers, ZZ Top, and Neil Diamond all have Harleys. Unfortunately, it seems that most movies tend to depict motorcycle riders as uncontrollable beasts and this has fed opinions offered by the media that all riders are outlaws. Fortunately, we know that is not true.*

It's only a matter of time before these posters will be collected both for their art and their place in American culture. Now is a good time to hop on board, while prices are still in first gear.

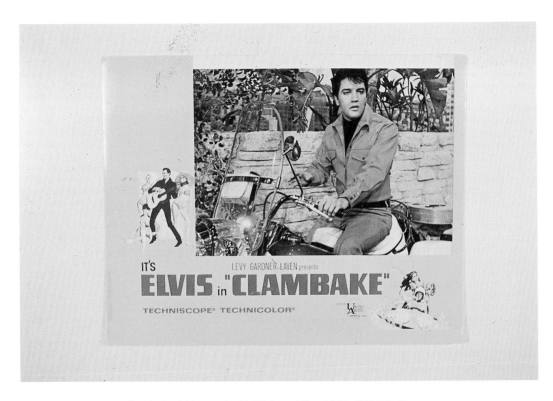

Clambake, lobby card with Elvis on bike, 1967. ($25-75) Courtesy of David Gaylin—Motorcycle Days.

Shampoo, lobby card with Warren Beatty on bike. ($10-25) *Courtesy of David Gaylin—Motorcycle Days.*

Little Fauss and Big Halsy, lobby card with bike scene, 1970. ($10-25) *Courtesy of David Gaylin—Motorcycle Days.*

Then Came Bronson, movie poster, copyright 1970, MGM. 27" x 41". ($50-150) *Courtesy of David Gaylin—Motorcycle Days.*

Motorcycle Gang, lobby card with bike scene, 1967. ($10-25) *Courtesy of David Gaylin—Motorcycle Days.*

Steve McQueen personality poster, jump scene from *The Great Escape*. The stunt was actually performed in the movie by longtime friend Bud Ekins. ($100-200) *Courtesy of David Gaylin—Motorcycle Days.*

The Wild Angels, one sheet, 1966. ($100-250) *Courtesy of David Gaylin—Motorcycle Days.*

Evel Knievel, one sheet, 1971. ($50-150) *Courtesy of David Gaylin—Motorcycle Days.*

Brigitte Bardot personality poster, 1960s. ($50-150) *Courtesy of David Gaylin—Motorcycle Days.*

Chapter 9

The Fast Track

Motorcycle Racing Memorabilia
Ken Sanders
Post World War I

Reliability runs, tourist trophies, endurance races, boardtrack racing, hill climbs, dirt track racing, speedways, Isle of Man, Savannah, Dodge City, Jack Pine, Daytona, Laconia. . . . and the occasional city street.

These are the places where racers, amateur and professional, official and unofficial, practiced the art of motorcycle racing. As with bicycles, motorcycle racing began soon after the first models rolled out of the "factories." Led by the experience and enthusiasm of two former bicycling champions, Oscar Hedstrom and George Hendee, Indian Motocycles dominated the racing circuits from 1902–1915, with Curtiss, Excelsior, Flying Merkel, Thor, and later Harley-Davidson as chief competitors.

The first races developed in the United States were reliability runs, where distance was more important than speed. It was truly a case of the well-tuned tortoise versus an oil splattering hare and, in the early rounds, the tortoise took the lead. Indian won the first United States endurance run, from Boston to New York, in 1902. A year later, Indian rider George N. Holden won the country's first long-distance track race at the Brighton Beach dirt track in New York City.

In 1906, Indian dealer Louis Mueller of Cleveland and George Holden of Springfield, Massachusetts, set a long-distance record, riding their new twin-cylinder Indians from New York to San Fransisco—3,476 miles—in thirty-one days, twelve hours, and thirteen minutes. This record would fall with a resounding thud, but it would take another five years to break it.

Early Indian racing stars included Stanley Kellogg and T. K. "Teddy" Hastings who, in 1907, won England's Thousand-mile Trial on his Indian (and would win again in 1908), the first entry of an American motorcycle in an English contest.

Meanwhile, another former bicycle maker, Glenn Curtiss, was taking the jackrabbit road, shooting for speed. In May 1903, Curtiss won the first American hill climb, sponsored by the New York Motorcycle Club. That summer he set a one-mile speed record in Providence, Rhode Island, pushing his bike to 63.8 miles per hour at a time when most top speeds were 40-45 miles per hour. In 1904, Curtiss ignited the history of Daytona-Ormond by setting a

ten-mile record on Ormond Beach, Florida, in eight minutes and fifty-four and two-fifths seconds. In 1905, in Syracuse, Curtiss set a record on dirt, doing one mile in one minute, one second.

In 1907, Curtiss brought his eight-cylinder, forty horsepower motorcycle to Ormond Beach, pushing it to 137 miles per hour, an unofficial world record. He spent the next two years routinely winning hill climbs and endurance races until the lure of aviation drew him away from motorcycle building. Still, Curtiss cycles would be sold in limited quantities up until World War I. With his racing successes and development of a powerful triple-cylinder motorcycle, it is hard to understand why Curtiss left, but it was to Indian's immediate advantage.

Reading Fairground motorcycle racing poster, unused, folded for mailing, 22" x 28". (Scarce—$100-250) *Courtesy of Dunbar Moonlight Kid Auctions.*

Somehow buried in obscurity while other riders such as Orrie
Steele, Albert "Shrimp" Burns, Cannonball Baker, and Bob Perry
got more publicity, Ken Sanders of Worcester, Massachusetts,
proved his mettle (and medals) as one of the leading endurance and
hill-climb racers from 1914-1922.

In 1908, riders and spectators wanted speed, speed, speed. Hedstrom designed an Indian with a loop frame specifically for racing. At the same time, an entrepreneur named Jack Prince opened the nation's first motordrome at the Coliseum in Los Angeles. A year later Hendee and Prince built a one-third mile motordrome in Springfield. Mile records dropped faster than a quart of oil.

The Indian star of this period was Jake DeRosier, who got his start by driving motorcycle pacers for bicycle races. For several exciting years, Jake won many boardtrack races and continually broke his own hundred-mile records in an exciting fashion, often running out of gas. DeRosier was fired from Indian in 1911 and moved over to Excelsior where he continued his winning ways. Unfortunately, like many racers, his luck ran out. In 1912, he was seriously injured in a bad accident while competing and subsequently died from complications in 1913.

Indian's greatest victories were landed in 1911 when their marque held every one of the 121 speed and distance records. Indian took the first three places in the prestigious Isle of Man races in England, and the company opened a sales office in London.

In 1912, the balance began to shift a bit. Because of the steep banking, slick boards made slicker by falling oil, and breakneck speeds, not to mention a lack of helmets, it was only a matter of time before disaster struck, and it did. A horrible accident in a Newark, New Jersey, motordrome left Indian rider Eddie Hasha and several spectators dead. The media now called the boardtracks "murderdromes."

Speedway, dirt track, endurance racing, and hill climbs were more popular. At the inaugural Dodge City 300 National Championship in 1914, Indian won, Thor took second, and Excelsior's Carly Goudy third.

The Excelsior Auto-Cycle pushed Indian. In 1912, at the Playa Del Rey Motordrome, Lee Humiston, on an Excelsior, became the first motorcyclist in the world to be officially timed at 100 miles per hour by a sanctioning organization. In 1915, riders Bob Perry and Carl Goudy took a number of wins, including the Chicago Speedway Park 300-mile event in record-setting time.

Harley-Davidson threw a leather helmet into the ring, fielding its first factory sponsored racing team at the 1914 Savannah, Georgia, 300-mile National Championship. Harley's Irving Janke finished third to Indian's Lee Taylor and Excelsior's Joe Wolters. The support drew almost immediate dividends, as Harley's Otto Walker won the 1915 Dodge City National Championships, a race in which Cyclone, Emblem, Excelsior, Harley, Indian, Merkel, and Pope had all entered teams. The racing balance had begun to swing Milwaukee way.

Who brought the Excelsior to the party? Can't tell if it's "Sandy" under the getup. What better way to spend Halloween? *Courtesy of the Dunbar Moonlight Kid Collection.*

Yonkers 24-hour endurance run perfect-score medal, Yonkers
Motorcycle Club, Ken Sanders, 1914. *Courtesy of the Dunbar
Moonlight Kid Collection.*

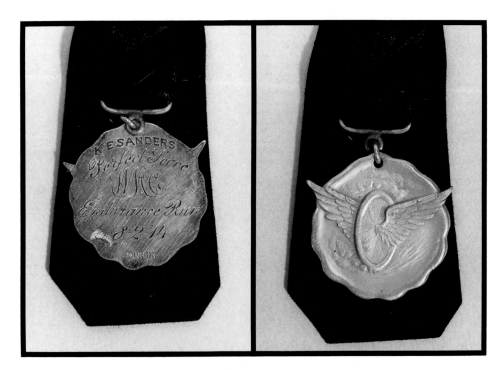

Worcester Motorcycle Club 24-hour endurance run perfect-score
medal, August 2, 1914, Ken Sanders. Note the Federation of
American Motorcyclists Winged Logo. "Sandy" owned the Worcester Motorcycle Club races for almost ten years. *Courtesy of the
Dunbar Moonlight Kid Collection.*

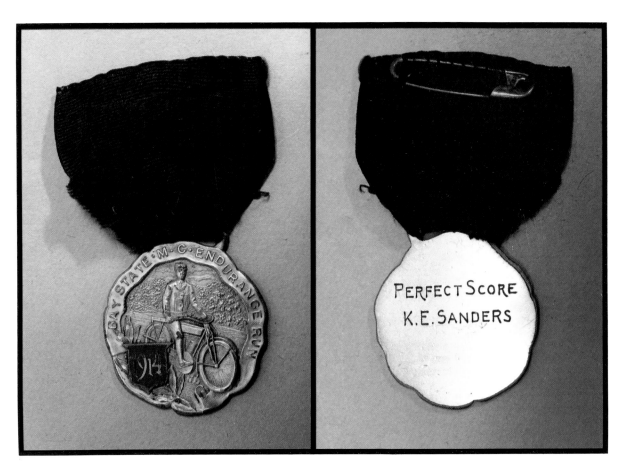

Bay State Motorcycle Club 24-hour endurance run perfect-score
medal, 1914, Ken Sanders. *Courtesy of the Dunbar Moonlight Kid
Collection.*

Worcester to Albany, New York, 24-hour endurance run perfect-
score medal, Worcester Motorcycle Club, 1000 points, Ken Sanders,
1914. *Courtesy of the Dunbar Moonlight Kid Collection.*

"Sandy" did all of his racing on Harley-Davidsons, either solos or sidecars. This was especially convenient for him as his good friend and sometime traveling companion, George Clift, owned the Harley agency in Worcester. Worcester, Massachusetts, Motorcycle Club 24-hour endurance run photo—left to right: John Lang, Fred Morin, Alan Frazelle, and Ken Sanders—August 2, 1914, 6" x 5". *Courtesy of the Dunbar Moonlight Kid Collection.*

Bay Ridge Long Island Motorcycle Club 210-mile endurance run perfect score medal, October 4, 1914. Yet another perfect score to cap a great rookie year for Ken Sanders. *Courtesy of the Dunbar Moonlight Kid Collection.*

Yonkers Motorcycle Club 24-hour endurance run perfect score medal, June 12-13, 1915. Ken Sanders won both individual high honors and was part of the team—with fellow Harley pro team members August Charlton of Jersey City, New Jersey, and Ralph Donaldson of Hoboken, New Jersey—first prize, with 2,943 points out of a possible 3,000, beating out Indian racers Orrie and John Steele. *Courtesy of the Dunbar Moonlight Kid Collection.*

1916 Worcester Motorcycle Championship trophy awarded to Ken Sanders. From the teens through the 1920s, Sanders was nearly unbeatable in his hometown. *Courtesy of the Dunbar Moonlight Kid Collection.*

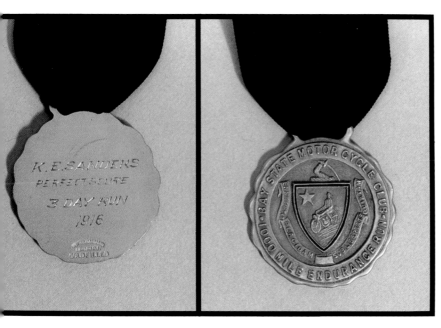

Bay State Motorcycle Club 1000 Endurance Run first place medal, Ken Sanders Sidecar Racing (Leon Laflamme in sidecar) for Harley Pro Team, first 1,000-mile race in motorcycling history. The rest of the Harley team didn't fare so well because of tire troubles. *Courtesy of the Dunbar Moonlight Kid Collection.*

Canadian Endurance Run Diamond medal, Ken Sanders and George Clift racing for the Harley team, June 10, 1916. The Sanders/Clift sidecar team beat out well-known endurance rider E. G. (Cannon-ball) Baker for first place. winning the diamond medal for Harley-Davidson. *Courtesy of the Dunbar Moonlight Kid Collection.*

Ken must have been a popular person at the 1916 Federation of American Motorcyclists Convention that took place in Providence, Rhode Island, July 26-29, 1916. *Courtesy of the Dunbar Moonlight Kid Collection.*

Sanders' scrapbook photos of him and George Clift during their Worcester to Canada odyssey. *Courtesy of the Dunbar Moonlight Kid Collection.*

Sandy first made headlines when he fearlessly delivered Worcester Gazettes from his Harley sidecar outfit during a New England blizzard. These scrapbook photos show the Gazette delivery fleet with Sandy and George Clift on their way to Canada and Sandy having fun with his Harley.

Photo of Ken Sanders, L. Herrington, and W. J. Ruhle, the Harley-Davidson team that won the team prize for the 1917 New Jersey Motorcycle Club 24-hour endurance run. Better known as the 10th Annual Eastern Road Championships, this was the most important run of the season. It was the only run in which the motorcycle manufacturers made entries. Harley handpicked its three riders and they did not disappoint—Ken scored 999 points out of 1,000. Unfortunately the gold and diamond medal that was awarded is the only award missing from this collection. *Courtesy of the Dunbar Moonlight Kid Collection.*

Harley, just getting into the racing game in 1914, started to make inroads into Indian's domination in 1915-16, a fact that they advertised whenever possible. *Courtesy of the Dunbar Moonlight Kid Collection.*

Worcester Motorcycle Club Championship watch, awarded to Ken Sanders, September 23, 1917. This was Ken's last race before he shipped off to France to keep the Allies' Harleys in top running condition. *Courtesy of the Dunbar Moonlight Kid Collection.*

Who was Kendall "Sandy" Sanders and why does it matter?

Good question. Ken Sanders, was a native of Worcester, Massachusetts, only half an hour from Indian hometown Springfield. He was a lifelong motorcycle enthusiast and a Harley-Davidson devotee. With boardtrack racing on the decline, hill climb, dirt track, and endurance races were the ones that the big makers counted upon for publicity.

How much did Ken love to ride motorcycles? In a scrapbook of clippings found in his estate collection, one 1915 article features Ken's unique method of delivering the *Worcester Telegram and Gazette* in his Harley with a specially rigged sidecar, in the *snow*. Obviously weather and road conditions did not deter the young Mr. Sanders, probably one of the reasons Harley-Davidson chose him for their racing team in 1915.

Ken first started racing in 1914, taking a perfect score in the Yonkers Motorcycle Club Endurance Run, a feat he duplicated in 1915. He also took home perfect scores in the Worcester and Bay State Motorcycle Club 24-hour endurance runs, and the Bay Ridge Long Island Motorcycle Club 210-mile Endurance Run.

In 1915, Ken helped Harley-Davidson solidify its new strength in racing. He won both the individual and team first prizes (with Ralph Donaldson of Hoboken, New Jersey, and August Charlton of Jersey City) in the June 1915 Yonkers 24-hour Endurance Run, beating out Indian stars Orrie and John Steele. Ken took home another Worcester 24-hour Endurance Run perfect score medal.

In May 1916, Ken won the first thousand-mile endurance motorcycle race ever run, from Boston to Buffalo and back, a arduous three-day affair that he shared with sidecar partner Leon LaFlamme, the only Harley team to finish with a perfect score. Harley heavily advertised this feat in *Motorcycling* and *Motorcycle Illustrated*, the feature trade publications of the day.

In June 1916, Ken and partner George Clift, the Worcester Harley-Davidson dealer, teamed up to win the diamond medal in a 477-mile Worcester-Canada endurance run, beating out the famous Cannonball Baker, who had recently set new transcontinental and Three Flags endurance records. Again the Harley team took home first place.

On May 30, 1917, Ken Sanders won the highest honors in professional motorcycling, winning both individual and team first places in the 1917 Eastern Road Championships, held in Newark, New Jersey. Harley-Davidson handpicked Ken, W. J. Ruhle of Jamaica, Long Island, and Arthur Herrington of Milwaukee, Wisconsin, to represent the company in this race. Harley also heavily advertised this victory, as Harley teams around the country began to be known as the "Wrecking Crew" for their numerous victories.

Ken finished the year in style, taking home his second straight pocket watch as Worcester Motorcycle Club Champion. In December, "Sandy" as he was also known, enlisted in the Harley-Davidson Overseas Unit, repairing Harley motorcycles in France for two years during World War I.

Upon his return in 1919, Ken wasted little time in setting a new hill climb record in the Worcester Club Hill climb. The next year he took home numerous trophies for Harley-Davidson, including first prizes in the New England Sectional Championship Hill climbs, both solo and sidecar divisions; in addition to solo and team prizes in the Massachusetts Motorcycle Association 24-hour Endurance Run.

In 1921, Ken's final year of extensive racing, he again set new hill climb records, defeating Orrie Steele and Albert "Shrimp" Burns, national Indian factory stars, among a dozen endurance and hill climb victories. In between races, Ken got married, taking (what else?) a honeymoon motorcycle tour with his new wife, Gertrude, before they moved to Boston.

The responsibilities of raising a family pre-empted any more serious racing, although Ken took home more hill climb trophies in 1922 and 1923. By 1924, the photos in the scrapbook had changed from fishing, racing, and touring outings to children on porch steps. A championship era had ended.

Ken never went anywhere without his Harley, be it fishing, swimming, or racing, he seemed to personify the rider who believed Harley's later slogan: "Motorcycling—The Greatest Sport in The World." *Courtesy of the Dunbar Moonlight Kid Collection.*

Fellow soldiers take a break for some hijinks. Sandy was stationed in Europe for two years as a Harley-Davidson mechanic. *Courtesy of the Dunbar Moonlight Kid Collection.*

Worcester Motorcycle Club hill climb first prize solo medal for Ken Sanders, September 27, 1919. Ken had just returned from tour in France and immediately returned to his pre-war form. *Courtesy of the Dunbar Moonlight Kid Collection.*

151

The joys of the open (?) road—Ken and friend navigating some muddy Worcester-area roads, circa 1919.

New England Sectional Climb first prize expert solo medal for Ken Sanders, September 18, 1920. *Courtesy of the Dunbar Moonlight Kid Collection.*

New England Sectional Climb first prize expert solo medal for Ken Sanders, September 18, 1920. *Courtesy of the Dunbar Moonlight Kid Collection.*

Ken and his Harley, probably at a race in Worcester, 1920, as well as other places in the 1920s. *Courtesy of the Dunbar Moonlight Kid Collection.*

1920 New England Sectional Hillclimb first-place trophy, solo division, June 20-21, 1920, Ken Sanders was equally adept at hill climbs and endurance runs and comfortable racing both solo and on sidecar Harleys. *Courtesy of the Dunbar Moonlight Kid Collection.*

Massachusetts Motorcycle Club team prize trophy, 24-hour endurance run, Ken Sanders, July 10-11, 1920, won with teammates H. B. Putnam, Fred Norquist, and John Lane. *Courtesy of the Dunbar Moonlight Kid Collection.*

As more and more makers dropped out of the motorcycle manufacturing game, it became a three-legged race—Harley, Indian, and Excelsior—with many racers running these makes as privateers, i.e., without factory support. With slumping sales, even Harley-Davidson pulled racing support for a few years, focusing instead on marketing. The American Motorcyclist Association competition committee did its best to keep out foreign competitors, but would be forced to acquiesce in the post World War II racing era.

The Jack Pine two-day, 500-mile Endurance Run made its debut in 1924. The first Daytona and Laconia races would be run in the late 1930s, all dominated by Harley and Indian, and later, contested by the invasion of British racers in the 1940s-50s.

Motorcycle racing memorabilia is among the most desirable of all collected. As it has been written many times in this book, the pre-World War I collectibles are particularly sought after, as the glory days of motorcycle racing. The older the pennants, racing jerseys, programs, trophies, fobs, medals, and pins, the better. Of course, national championship awards with provenance are better than local awards with no provenance. Anything to do with long-running, well-known races such as Dodge City, Daytona, Laconia, etc.. Also, short-lived, lesser-known races and material concerning the boardtracks is also wanted. Motorcycle collectors appreciate knowledge about all aspects of the sport, from the races to the motorcycles to the racers themselves.

Early material that features obscure motorcycles such as Cyclone, Curtiss, Emblem, Flying Merkel, Pope, and Thor are particularly in demand as there is simply so little

that is known to exist. Similarly, material regarding the short-lived 1930s Crocker cycles is also coveted.

Longtime experts Jerry Hatfield and Stephen Wright have written extensively about motorcycle racing and the stars of various eras. However, as seen in the case of Kendall Sanders, it is possible to find racing champions of note who were heretofore undocumented in books, even though their contributions are undisputed.

I did not place individual values on the Sanders collection, as with this complete grouping of one man's racing career it is impossible to put a separate value on each piece. However, if these medals belonged to separate racers, I would guesstimate (yes, a combination of guessing and estimating) that the medals and the trophies would be worth $150-$400 each, depending on the race and competitors, maybe more. It's difficult to find out all that information, which also makes the Sanders collection more interesting, in that all of his victories are documented in both magazine and newspaper clippings and in photos in his own personal scrapbook. As Ken was a lifelong motorcyclist, the scrapbook also includes hundreds of photos taken of him and his friends on various outings, with most riding Harley-Davidsons.

The prices given in this chapter, as in the rest of this book, are only to be used as guidelines. Collections are generally worth more than single pieces, because collections give a more comprehensive view of a racer or race. Again, usually the earlier the piece, the better; the better the condition, the higher the price; the scarcer the item, the more value placed on it.

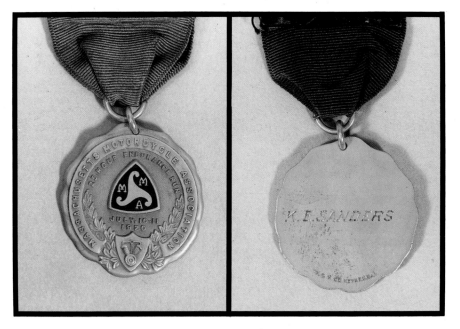

Massachusetts Motorcycle Association 25-hour endurance run perfect-score medal, Ken Sanders, July 10-11, 1920. Endurance runs didn't have quite the amount of danger as board track racing, and Americans were obsessed in the 1920s with getting from point A to point B in the absolute shortest amount of time. *Courtesy of the Dunbar Moonlight Kid Collection.*

Massachusetts Motorcycle Association Worcester hill climb first-prize medal, April 19, 1921, sidecar class, Ken Sanders. Orrie Steele sets a solo record on Chandler Hill, but Ken retains his sidecar title. *Courtesy of the Dunbar Moonlight Kid Collection.*

First-prize trophy for American Motorcyclist Association open hill climb, Merrimack Valley Motorcycle Club of Lowell, Massachusetts, sidecar class, Ken Sanders, May 30, 1921. *Courtesy of the Dunbar Moonlight Kid Collection.*

Hosmer Mountain hill climb first-prize trophy, Willimantic, Connecticut, Ken Sanders, September 21, 1921. Ken won both the 72- and 80-inch classes. *Courtesy of the Dunbar Moonlight Kid Collection.*

Hosmer Mountain hill climb first-prize trophy, Willimantic, Connecticut, Ken Sanders, September 21, 1921. Ken won both the 72- and 80-inch classes. *Courtesy of the Dunbar Moonlight Kid Collection.*

Massachusetts Motorcycle Club, Worcester Hill Climb expert sidecar first-prize medal, October 12, 1921. Ken set a side-car record of 16.8 seconds. *Courtesy of the Dunbar Moonlight Kid Collection.*

Massachusetts Motorcycle Association hill climb medal, awarded to Ken Sanders, 1922. *Courtesy of the Dunbar Moonlight Kid Collection.*

Judging by the rest of his life, how else would Sandy marry but on a Harley side-car outfit? *Courtesy of the Dunbar Moonlight Kid Collection.*

1923 Massachusetts Motorcycle Association Club Team Prize, Worcester Hill Climb, April 191, 1923, Ken Sanders. *Courtesy of the Dunbar Moonlight Kid Collection.*

Pair of Indian trophies, circa 1920. In Ken Sander's collection, picking up these factory trophies must have caused some consternation amongst his Wigwam competitors.
Courtesy of the Dunbar Moonlight Kid Collection.

American Motorcyclist Association, 1929 Gypsy Tour medal, Ken Sanders. After marriage, a move to the Boston area, and children, Ken still found time to ride with friends. *Courtesy of the Dunbar Moonlight Kid Collection.*

One of the earliest motorcycle races, New York Motorcycle Club, Reliability Run ribbon, November 3, 1903. The first United States endurance run took place from Boston to New York on July 4-5, 1902. On September 5, 1903, George Holden, the first Indian dealer, won the first motorcycle long-distance track race at the Brighton Beach dirt track of New York City, covering 150 miles in the allotted four hours with an average speed of 35 miles per hour. 6" x 2 1/2". (Rare—$100-300) *Courtesy of Dunbar Moonlight Kid Auctions.*

Sandy and child, circa 1925, different priorities for the family man. *Courtesy of the Dunbar Moonlight Kid Collection.*

Harley-Davidson Loving Cup Trophy, circa 1920, sterling silver with wood base, 15" tall. ($100-200) *Courtesy of Dunbar Moonlight Kid Auctions.*

Motorcycle Reliability Trials, Indian Trophy Loving Cup Trophy, October 11-12, 1924, awarded to Adolph Miller, solo class, sterling silver with wood base, 14" tall. ($100-300) *Courtesy of Dunbar Moonlight Kid Auctions.*

Wool Harley-Davidson racing sweater, circa 1920s, "Electa" on sleeve. Harley was a relatively late entrant into the racing game. On November 26, 1914, Harley entered its first factory sponsored team in the Savannah 300 National Championship, finishing third. Harley moved up the Big Three ladder in 1915, as rider Otto Walker won the Second Dodge City 300, thus beginning a seven-year run for the Harley "Wrecking Crew." (Scarce—$100-500) *Courtesy of the Dunbar Moonlight Kid Aucton.*

Program for the 1926 Championship Motorcycle Races at Rockingham Motor Speedway, lists riders such as Johnny Seymour and Joe Petrali. Petrali split his racing time between Harley and Excelsior, especially after Harley withdrew support from racing. However, Harley hired Joe as an engineer, and he made many improvements in the Big Twins for the company in the 1930s. The star of this race meet, however, was Curly Fredericks riding an Indian "61" side valve. He registered the fastest lap ever turned on the boards at 120.3 miles per hour, a record which has never been broken. ($30-75) *Courtesy of the Dunbar Moonlight Kid Collection.*

Oval dirt track racer's iron shoe, hand made with sheet iron for the left foot and leather-riveted, adjustable buckled belt to protect racers' toes from the track during the lean. Circa 1930s. ($30-75) *Courtesy of the Dunbar Moonlight Kid Collection.*

Souvenir program from the 22nd Annual Gypsy Tour, 1938, in Athol, Massachusetts. Includes many motorcycle dealers ads, some graphic photos, race poses, action cover. 36 pages, 6" x 8 1/2", *Courtesy of the Dunbar Moonlight Kid Collection.* $30-75

A lot of the best riders would spend their Saturday nights at Bulkeley Stadium. Four motorcycle racing programs from Hartford Bulkeley Stadium, 1936, featuring Woodsie Castanguay, Lou Wilson, Kenny Brower, and Jimmy Dummit on the covers with stories about each racer and autographs in each program. Each 10 pages, 6" x 9". (Overall excellent condition— $30-75 each) *Courtesy of Dunbar Moonlight Kid Auctions.*

Assorted Radio Type news reports from Harley-Davidson, with
weekly Racing results from 1938-40 countrywide. Notice that
competitors' brand names are blanked out. 8" x 11". ($5-15 each)
Courtesy of the Dunbar Moonlight Kid Collection.

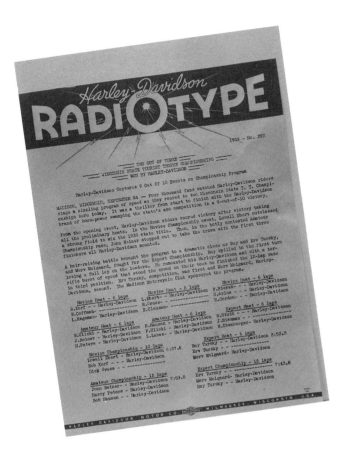

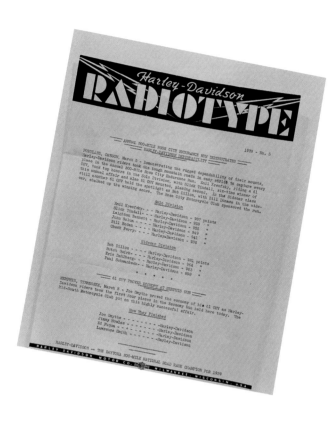

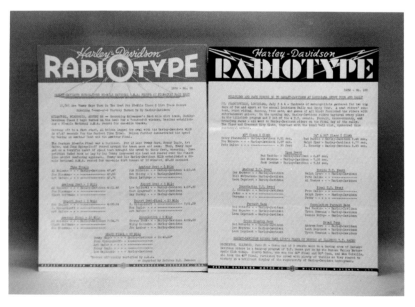

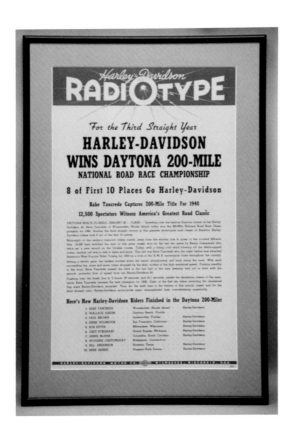

Framed 1940 Radio Type poster announcing 80 first-place Harley-Davidson wins at the Daytona 300. Indian's Ed Kretz won the inaugural Daytona 200 on the beach in 1937—the same year Joe Petrali took a Knucklehead "61" down to the sand and broke Indian rider Johnny Seymour's 11-year American record of 136 miles per hour. In 1940, Harley brought out the WDLR model and rider Arthur "Babe" Tancrede of Rhode Island won both Daytona and the Laconia 100 National Championship. 10 1/2" x 16 1/2". ($50-125) *Courtesy of Bob "Sprocket" Eckardt.*

Programs from night raacing at Hartford Bulkeley Stadium Programs with Dutch Mueller, Joe Sypeck, Jimmie Gibb, and Stanley Lipskey on the covers as well as a photo of the stadium. Inside are many racers signatures including Woodsie Castenguay, Bud McCrea, and Lou Wilson. A great early reference. Each 10 pages, 1936-1938, 6" x 9". ($30-75) *Courtesy of Dunbar Moonlight Kid Auctions.*

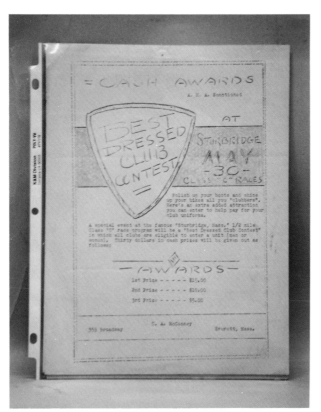

A group of historical reference materials from 1939 including a Gypsy Tour Booklet with 23rd Annual, 100 Laconia, National Tourist Trophy Championships, a welcome brochure, schedule maps, list of entrants, welcome letter from New Hampshire's governor to the president of the state's motorcycle dealer association announcing a contest for "Miss Motorcyclist of 1939," a best-dressed-club contest sheet, and a Safety Convention announcement, 8" x 11". ($30-75 Group) *Courtesy of the Dunbar Moonlight Kid Collection.*

Pennant from the 1938 Laconia National Championship motorcycle races. Harley took home the gold again. 15 1/2" x 6". ($50-150) *Courtesy of Dunbar Moonlight Kid Auctions.*

This was one of the few hillclimbs not won by Excelsior rider Gene Rhyne in 1930. Indian Scout "45" poster with Swede Mattson in action hill-climb photo, 19" x 25". ($100-350) *Courtesy of the Dunbar Moonlight Kid Collection.*

Harley-Davidson 1940 Class "A" hill-climb poster picturing action at Mount Garfield, unused, folded for mailing to dealers, 37" x 24". ($100-400) *Courtesy of Dunbar Moonlight Kid Auctions.*

Two-hundred-mile National Championship pin from Laconia, New Hampshire, gold plated and stamped "Robbins Co. Attleboro" (Mass.) on reverse side, 1938, 1 1/4" long. ($25-85) *Courtesy of Bob "Sprocket" Eckardt.*

Flyer advertises hill climb competition in North Guilford, Connecticut, sanctioned by the American Motorcyclist Association. 14" x 21". ($50-150) *Courtesy of Dunbar Moonlight Kid Auctions.*

Harley-Davidson celebrated a string of Jack Pine wins with this 1940 poster featuring Ted Konecny, winner; and Dot Robinson, class A sidecar winner. Unused condition, folded for mailing to dealers. ($100-400) *Courtesy of Dunbar Moonlight Kid Auctions.*

Harley-Davidson 200-mile Speedway Championship poster, 1940, featuring winner Louis Guanella and twelve insert photos of action and people. Guanella won the race using a spare motor built by master tuner Tom Sifton in just a few days. His speed, 84.64 miles per hour, was the highest average speed yet for a Class C "stock" motorcycle race. 37" x 24". ($100-400) *Courtesy of Dunbar Moonlight Kid Auctions.*

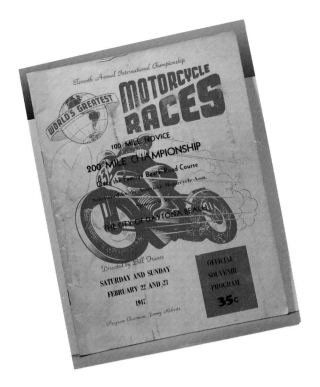

The official program from the 1947, eleventh annual Daytona 200-mile Championship race, featuring a 1947 Indian ad, racing scenes, party scenes, and lists of race participants. This is a scarce program since this was the first post–World War II Daytona race to be held. Johnny Spiegelhoff, who changed his colors from green to Injun red, won the 200-mile expert division. ($50-100) *Courtesy of the Dunbar Moonlight Kid Collection.*

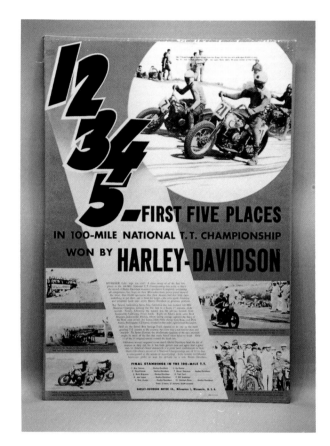

Harley-Davidson Poster celebrating the top-five winners of the National Tourist Trophy Championship in Riverside, California. Longtime Harley man Ray Tanner took home top honors, with Floyd Emde a close second. Harley captured the top-five places. Indian was becoming less and less of a factor, but Norton, BSA, and other British makes were beginning to make their presence known stateside. These posters have been reproduced, but this is an original. 1947. 27" x 41". ($100-400) *Courtesy of the Dunbar Moonlight Kid Collection.*

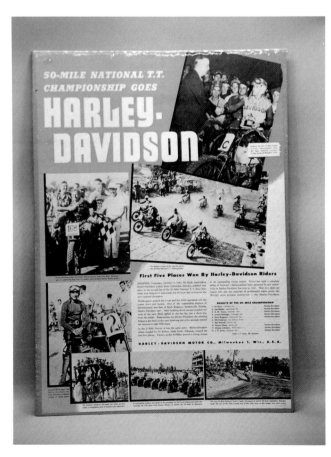

Harley-Davidson racing poster featuring the Memphis, Tennessee, 1947 National 50-mile Tourist Trophy Championship. These posters have been reproduced, but this is an original. Posters like this one-sheet racing poster are much more desirable than the banner-style posters because they offer greater color, size, and action. 27" x 41". ($100-400) *Courtesy of the Dunbar Moonlight Kid Collection.*

Harley won nineteen of twenty-three national titles in 1948, the remaining four were won by Indian. Jimmy Chann took his second straight Springfield, Illinois, title. It's Harley-Davidson "Again" in this August 1948 poster with original mailer, 34" x 11". ($50-100) *Courtesy of Dunbar Moonlight Kid Auctions.*

Sam Arena, just retired from road racing, conquers the hills of San Jose, California with a win in the 45" expert class. "Go Harley-Davidson" hill-climb poster, September 1948, 34" x 11". ($50-100) *Courtesy of Dunbar Moonlight Kid Auctions.*

Joe Weatherly repeats his 1948 flat track feats and it's a Harley Laconia love-in, with nine of the first ten places going to the Milwaukee racers. Promoting its racing victories, Harley invited customers to be winners by association. "Harley-Davidson Wins Again" Poster, 100 Mile National Road Race Championship, Laconia, June 1949, 34" x 11". ($50-100) *Courtesy of Dunbar Moonlight Kid Auctions.*

Although the factories were concentrating more on speed championships instead of hill climbing, Harleys still dominated the 1948 season, both in A and C classes. "Harley-Davidson Wins" hill-climb poster, August 1948, *Courtesy of Dunbar Moonlight Kid Auctions.*

With the introduction of the model KR in August, available both as a dirt-tracker and a road-racer, and a top speed of 150, other makers spent the next seventeen years trying to catch up. Harley-Davidson poster "Brashear on a KR Wins," 1952 5-Mile National Championship, 24" x 18". ($100-400) *Courtesy of Dunbar Moonlight Kid Auctions.*

Charles Daniels brought home Harley's fourth consecutive Laconia checkered flag. Pennants like this are very sought after as so many were thrown out with baseball card collections, or chewed on by non-motoring mice and moths. Laconia Gypsy Tour Pennant, 1939, 23" long. ($50-200) *Courtesy of Dunbar Moonlight Kid Auctions.*

This pennant is probably a souvenir of a Laconia Bike Week in New Hampshire, 3 1/2" x 8" on 10"-stick, circa 1950. ($50-150) *Courtesy of the Dunbar Moonlight Kid Collection.*

Laconia National Championship Road Race notebook, 1958, 2 1/2" x 6". This was the first postwar year where Harley failed to win the majority of national events. ($50-100) *Courtesy of the Dunbar Moonlight Kid Collection.*

At the grandaddy of them all, Dodge City, celebrating 42 years of racing. Harley-Davidson cloth jacket patch, 1956, 4 1/2" x 2 1/2". ($50-100) *Courtesy of Bob "Sprocket" Eckardt.*

At Daytona they raced (and partied) on the beach until 1961. It is now the spring break of choice for thousands of bikers who travel from all over the globe to check out each others' chrome and pipes, and to catch a race or two. Daytona Beach National Championship Races poster, circa 1950s, shrinkwrapped, 15" x 22". ($100-400) *Courtesy of Dunbar Moonlight Kid Auctions.*

Wisconsin Centennial Exposition National Championship Motorcycle Races poster, circa 1950s, 22" x 33". ($150-500) *Courtesy of Dunbar Moonlight Kid Auctions.*

A giveaway for contestants in the National Jack Pine Run in Lansing, Michigan, a rugged test of endurance begun in 1925. These cowbells were given to all hardy contestants. The winner, of course, got the big cowbell inscribed with his name. 1959, with belt and buckle, 1 1/2" x 1 1/2", belt 3". ($25-75) *Courtesy of Dunbar Moonlight Kid Auctions.*

Hill climb programs for 1950s Jolly Rogers races in Seattle, Washington—May 1951, April 1952, June 1952, Sept 1954, and May 1957. All have many ads including Indian and Harley dealers. Each 10 pages with graphic covers. 6" x 9". ($25-75 Group) *Courtesy of Dunbar Moonlight Kid Auctions.*

Motorcycle Scrambles poster, circa 1950s, in original mailing tube, 14" x 21". ($50-100) *Courtesy of Dunbar Moonlight Kid Auctions.*

Cardboard storecard of hill climb at Feura Bush, New York, with photo insert of rider on an Indian wearing Indian racing shirt. ($50-100) *Courtesy of Dunbar Moonlight Kid Auctions.*

Trophies from Aggie Run and Drag, 1955, 12" tall ($25-75) and from Arlene's Third Annual MM Poker Run, 1958, 13" tall, ($25-75) *Courtesy of Bob "Sprocket" Eckardt.*

Shawnee Creeper High Point trophy, 1962, 8" x 20" x 3". ($25-75) *Courtesy of the Dunbar Moonlight Kid Collection.*

Pat Imes's trophy from the Second Annual Dot Robinson Run, April 28, 1957, 4 1/2" x 7" x 3". ($25-75) *Courtesy of the Dunbar Moonlight Kid Collection.*

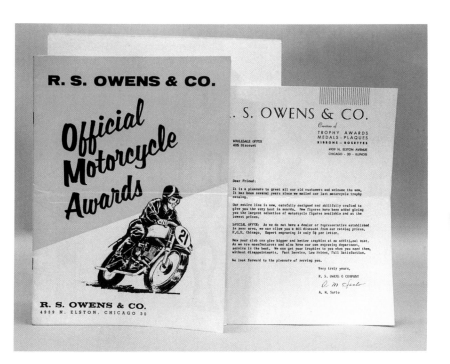

R. S. Owens Trophy Company *Official Motorcycle Awards* catalog
with twenty pages of sports, trophies, and jewelery, 1958, 8" x 11".
($10-30) *Courtesy of the Dunbar Moonlight Kid Collection.*

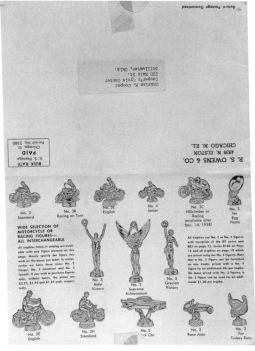

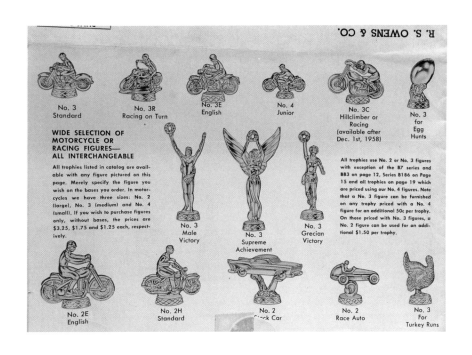

Chapter 10
Accessories Make the Outfit
Miscellaneous Motorcycle Toys and Extras

Some of you may think that Elvis or Fonzie were the first to wear leather jackets and start that cool biker's fashion trend which remains hot forty odd years later.

In actuality, leather lore dates the birth of this fashion statement to shortly after the first official wipeout caused by slipping on some horse exhaust and falling hard and long (not to mention deep). Those in the know decided to take some horse kin, being cow skin, the most absorbent of scrapes and scratches, stitch it together, making it the biker's armor against pavement.

A cycling apparel tradition was born. To prove this theory, one needn't look any further than early accessories catalogs (see Chapters 4-6), going back to the motor-bike infancy of cycling. Industrial age entrepreneurs have spent the last ninety years or so trying to make the population look fashionable on bike-back, while protecting the biker from the hazards of motorcycle mechanical idiosyncrasies and cruelties of the road.

In the Excelsior Auto-Cycle catalog of 1912, on page 25, one could choose a leather coat with mandarin style collar or a Russian vest to slip over one's shirt and tie. Long leather gloves extended from fingertips to forearm. And if that was not enough protection, how about a rubber motor shirt and/or a full-length duster? Very useful in the rain and also for those wonderful total-loss oil systems where the oil just goes through and, splat, comes out the other end. Good thing that goggles were also developed for the new motoring generation.

Another favorite of riders were leather leggings, or putties. These were worn on the calves for those tight curves when the bike leaned low. How low? So low that sparks would fly off of the metal fasteners.

Harley-Davidson has understood the value of riders' accessories for most of the company's existence. Since the early days of the company's 94-year history, Harley has put out a genuine Harley accessories catalog, offering the motorcycle enthusiast every possible item from clothing to pennants to pins to fobs to windshields, tools, paints, and much, much more. In the 1937 Harley catalog, swatches of material are even shown so that motorcyclists can choose the colors of their Twillardine shirts and breeches. Don't forget the bow tie and the monogrammed "Sonny" over the

From the early 1900s to World War I, Motorcycle manufacturers and publications promoted motorcycling as a combination of cheap transportation and a wholesome but exciting sport. *Courtesy of the Dunbar Moonlight Kid Collection.*

breast pocket. Top off the outfit with a "Classy Cap" and you're ready to impress the ladies!

Speaking of ladies, companies did not ignore the feminine part of the population, even though Harley literature insisted for years upon mostly placing them in the sidecars of their new models. Specially designed leather jackets, with more pockets and better styling can be seen in the Harley ad in the March 1954 issue of Motorcycling Magazine. Women also could choose the special "Cyclette" cap that they could tie under their chins, just like one of those rain hats that insurance companies used to give out! When the women's motorcycling organization, the Motor Maids, was formed in 1941, they searched for a uniform look and ended up choosing one that was very similar to their male counterparts—blue button-down shirt with Motor Maids embroidered on the back, naugahyde tie, gray trousers, white belt, and saddle shoes or boots. Kind of like their sister lovely Rita the Meter Maid. No wonder they rode fast.

Motorcycle manufacturers emphasized the importance of neat dressing. Even before the advent of biker gangs, motorcyclists could get a bad rap from those who chose to ride recklessly or let the pipes burst a machine gun staccato. The companies had to appeal to the middle class so they would buy cycles to tour, hunt, fish, swim, or have a good time simply getting from point A to point B. Their advertising and customer publications always pictured the motorcyclist at his best.

Henry Ford's assembly line technology and subsequent price reductions in cars made the motorcycle market a tough one in which to succeed. From a high of several hundred manufacturers in 1912, the evidence shows that only two American cycle makers survived World War II. Only one stands today—Harley-Davidson. For some reason, Indian never offered the same line of accessories as Harley. I've only seen a couple of catalogs, including a crude 1959 catalog, long after they were bought out by the English company Enfield. Note the smiling gent checking his cuffs in the Indian "New 10 Star Racing Shirt"(see Chapter 5). No wonder the company went down the pipes.

Motorcycle accessories have really changed very little during this century. The major change has been the mandating of helmets. Go into any Harley dealership and you'll see a herd of leather jackets and pants, mostly black, cool sunglasses, and some crushing boots. Of course, if you want the ultimate accessories, you can pony up a few grand for a Harley CD jukebox or Harley pinball machine. And, you won't have to worry about either getting caught in your chain.

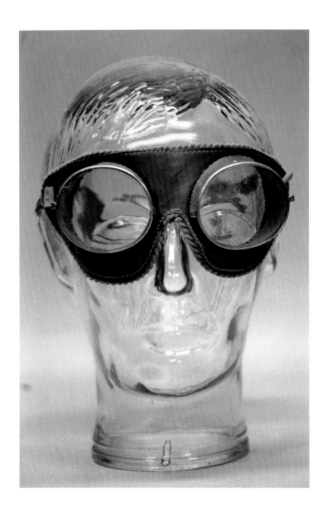

Motorcycle goggles, circa 1920s. ($20-50) *Courtesy of the Dunbar Moonlight Kid Collection.*

Pair of leather putties, circa 1915. Leather has always been the protective cloth of choice for cycling enthusiast. Putties offered some relief from flying rocks and low cornering. ($50-100*) Courtesy of Dunbar Moonlight Kid Auctions.*

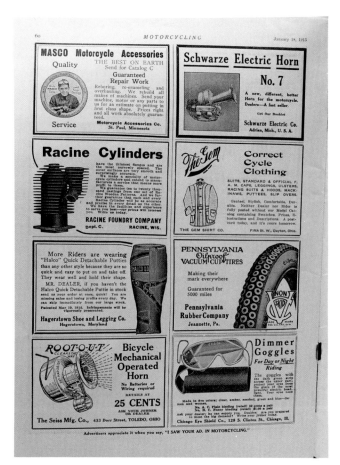

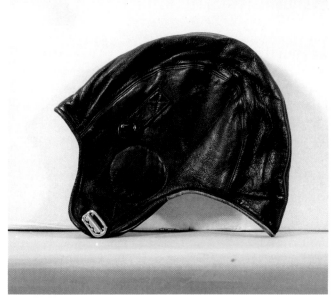

Harley leather rider's cap, circa 1940s-50s. ($50-100) *Courtesy of the Dunbar Moonlight Kid Collection.*

Ad for Halco Detachable Leather Putties in *Motorcycling* magazine, January 18, 1915.

Incised leather kidney belt, circa 1950s. ($50-125) *Courtesy of the Dunbar Moonlight Kid Collection.*

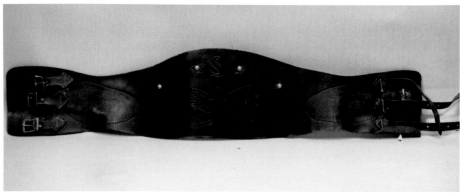

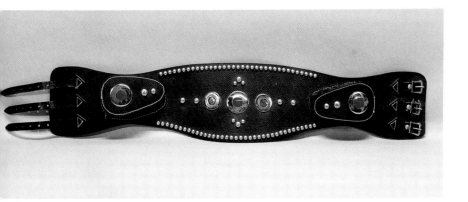

Leather kidney belt with reflectors, circa 1950s. ($50-125) *Courtesy of the Dunbar Moonlight Kid Collection.*

White Harley jacket, circa 1970s. ($25-50) *Courtesy of the Dunbar Moonlight Kid Collection.*

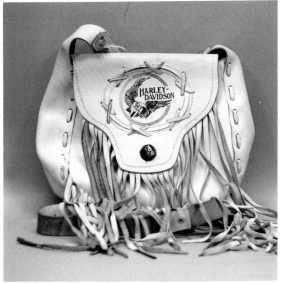

Harley-Davidson white leather pocketbook with fringe, circa 1960s. ($50-125) *Courtesy of the Dunbar Moonlight Kid Collection.*

Wichita Jeep Motorcycle Club shirt, features cartoon character from Popeye strip. ($25-75) *Courtesy of the Dunbar Moonlight Kid Collection.*

176

Black Panthers Motorcycle Club denim vest, circa 1960s, from Philadelphia, Pennsylvania. ($50-100) *Courtesy of the Dunbar Moonlight Kid Collection.*

Kentucky Ramblers Shirt, circa 1950s. ($25-75) *Courtesy of the Dunbar Moonlight Kid Collection.*

Harley-Davidson racing club jacket, Tulsa, Oklahoma, circa 1950s, with policeman on back. ($50-125) *Courtesy of Dunbar Moonlight Kid Auctions.*

Harley-Davidson leather visor. ($10-30) *Courtesy of the Dunbar Moonlight Kid Collection.*

Indian saddle bag, circa 1940s. 14" x 9". ($50-100) *Courtesy of the Dunbar Moonlight Kid Collection.*

Massachusetts porcelain motorcycle license plate, 1915. (Rare in porcelain—$50-100) *Courtesy of the Dunbar Moonlight Kid Collection.*

Maine motorcycle license plate, 1948, 6" x 4 1/2", unused in original envelope. ($50-100) *Courtesy of the Dunbar Moonlight Kid Collection.*

Indiana motorcycle license plate, 1962. ($10-30) *Courtesy of the Dunbar Moonlight Kid Collection.*

Pennsylvania motorcycle license plates dated 1963; 1952, 1945, and 1930, 7" x 4". ($10-20 each) *Courtesy of the Dunbar Moonlight Kid Collection.*

Pair of Harley-Davidson tanks, original, 20"
long. ($50-100) *Courtesy of the Dunbar
Moonlight Kid Collection.*

Harley-Davidson spark plug, circa 1950s, in
original box. ($10-30) *Courtesy of the
Dunbar Moonlight Kid Collection.*

Pocket mirror, oval, showing smiling cop on
duty on his motorcycle, 2" x 3". ($25-75)
*Courtesy of the Dunbar Moonlight Kid
Collection.*

Harley-Davidson #3 spark plug, in original
box. ($10-30) *Courtesy of the Dunbar
Moonlight Kid Collection.*

Toys

(AUTHOR'S NOTE: *In the first volume of Motorcycle Collectibles, American cast-iron toys were covered thoroughly. The following toys were not available for the first book, but hold a lot of interest for both casual and avid collectors. Some are not of American origin, but add so much color and flair that I had to include them. However, for background material, I did choose to add some information regarding the cast iron toys, as they are among the most valuable and desirable of all motorcycle toys. In a future volume, I may discuss tin motorcycle toys in detail. However, as most were made in foreign countries (i.e., Germany, Japan, and England) I didn't think they would fit into a book that has almost a complete American focus.*

The most famous American tin motorcycle toys were made by Marx in the 1920s-40s. The best-known and loved cast-iron toys were made by Hubley Manufacturing of Lancaster, Pennsylvania. For photos and pricing information regarding the toys mentioned in this introduction, please refer to Motorcycle Collectibles, Volume I.

In the 1930s, the Hubley and Arcade companies fought a cast-iron toy battle equivalent of the Hatfields and McCoys feud. Arcade, out of Freeport, Illinois, forged toys under their motto of "They look real." Hubley, from Lancaster, Pennsylvania, rolled out their yearly line with the caption "They look like the real ones."

Both companies raced to sign up full-size vehicle makers for the exclusive contract to recreate their work in miniature. Arcade, the king of cast iron, built beautiful replicas of yellow cabs, farm tractors, sporty Reo coupes, and intricate Packard roadsters. Hubley, the prince, managed to beat out Arcade for the right to work the two-wheeled side of the street, making Indian and Harley toy cycles for rider tots.

Hubley's Indian line, full of delivery, crime-fighting, and service vehicles, portrayed the era's most exciting action, from the dependability of the U.S. Postal Service to a thrilling gangster chase via an armored cycle. Even during the Depression, Hubley could give a receptive public lifelike toys at affordable prices. The company offered the smallest toys for as little as 10-25 cents or as much as $5-8. As the largest-size toys were the most costly to manufacture, they were the most expensive to buy, which contributes to their scarcity today.

In 1996, cast-iron toy collectors and vintage cycle lovers both covet the small-scale bikes. Like most other collectibles, cast iron motorcycle prices have accelerated like a Daytona straightaway over the past several years. The toys that bring the most money are the rarest ones with the most paint. The Indian cop cycle, bought for cousin Hubert but kept out of reach in the china closet is now worth a hell of a lot more (hundreds to thousands of dollars) than the one Joey raced on the hot top for hours.

All the prices quoted here are in a wide range, depending on whether Joey, Hubert, or the more moderate Marvin got their hands on the toys first. Missing or replaced handlebars, tires, and drivers all lessen the price, and repainted toys have practically no value.

Most of the Indian cycles are painted in the trademark red, Harleys are draped with a coat of the military gray drab adopted by the company during World War I, although the smaller bikes were dipped in a splash guard of colors. Beginning collectors can buy four-inch Indian crash cars with molded drivers for $100-$375, or seven-inch Indian crash cars for $300-$800. On the Harley side of the road, five-and-a-half-inch cop cycles will sell between $150-$500 and civilian models, with a sporty cap, for $200-$800. Note that mint condition cycles sell for whatever the market bears at the time.

Moving into larger bikes, kids could play cops and robbers with their nine-inch Indian Armored Car, with cop driver and sidecar passenger protected from the rounds fired from Dillinger or Capone. Or they could be the lone rider, speeding an Indian four-cylinder, nine-inch solo cycle to the scene of the crime. Today, a complete Armored Car sells for anywhere between $1,000-3,000, a four-cylinder cycle between $400-$1,500.

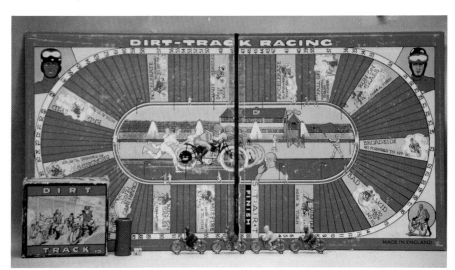

Bell's Dirt Track Racing board game, circa 1920s, England, complete with box, board, dice and four cast motorcycles; board 24" x 12". ($100-250) *Courtesy of the Dunbar Moonlight Kid Collection.*

Not only did Indian cycles work to protect and serve, they moved the mail and helped the country's fledgling road system. Hubley's eleven-inch U.S. Mail Delivery has all the features of the real thing except the letters themselves. Even larger, the detailed twelve-inch Indian traffic and crash cars are highly desired by collectors. Real life traffic cars were used to expedite equipment and lights. Crash cars, equipped with axes, hosereel, and canisters, raced to accident scenes to aid injured motorists and disabled vehicles. The toy versions certainly top their counterparts' original price tags—the Traffic Car, when found, will change hands between $2,500-$7,500, the Crash Car between $2,000-$6,000.

Hubley's Harley-Davidson king-size line is led by a trio of large bikes, all in olive. Exports and sales of cycles to local police departments helped to keep Harley in business during The Depression. Harley Cop Solo cycles are sold in the range of $500-$1,500, depending on the level of paint; a Harley Cop with Sidecar is $800-$2,200 with both rider and passenger in super condition. The Parcel Post was Hubley's representation of the Harley Servi-Car delivery line, with the responsibility of delivering packages promptly and reliability.

For those who want the best of the best, the Hubley "Say it with Flowers" Delivery Van is it. Unlike most of the Indian motorcycles, its color is an unusual turquoise blue. Hubley distributed it in five different sizes, so kids with all-size pockets could afford an example. Yet all the sizes are very difficult for collectors to track down. The smallest size cycle can sell for anywhere between $800-$2,500, and the prices climb to the largest, eleven-inch size, "Flowers," which runs between $5,000-$25,000. That could also buy a very nice, full-size Scout. For a short time, Hubley even built a motorized version, with a key wind mechanism.

Hubley made cast-iron toy cycles right up to World War II, until raw material shortages and scrap drives changed the course of their business. Indian didn't outlast the war by many years, either. And we all know that Harley rules the road today. But the eternal bond between Hubley, Indian, and Harley strengthens each time another small cycle rolls out of the sandbox and onto the shelf.

Bell's Dirt Track racing board game, 1940s version, withboard and plastic figures, 12" x 12". ($50-150) *Courtesy of the Dunbar Moonlight Kid Collection.*

Motorcycle playing cards, circa 1920s, made in Belgium. ($50-100) *Courtesy of the Dunbar Moonlight Kid Collection.*

This tin "Atom" bike from Japan is the best battery operated motorcycle toy I've seen, circa 1950s. You turn the bike on, it revs up, runs, and the rider gets on and off. 12" long. ($300-900) *Courtesy of the Dunbar Moonlight Kid Collection.*

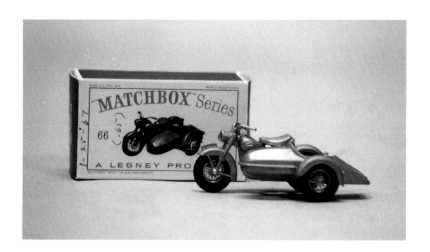

Matchbox Harley-Davidson motorcycle and sidecar, circa 1966, 3" long. ($50-150) *Courtesy of the Dunbar Moonlight Kid Collection.*

Moto-Cross Game, French, 1960s. ($50-100) *Courtesy of the Dunbar Moonlight Kid Collection.*

Harley plastic solo bike with removable rider, 1940s, Acme, (Rare with rider—$10-50) *Courtesy of the Dunbar Moonlight Kid Collection.*

Plastic racing motorcycle with sidecar, 1960s, Sonsco, Hong Kong, with box, 4 1/4" long. ($50-150) *Courtesy of the Dunbar Moonlight Kid Collection.*

184

Tin windup sedan and motorcycle from West Germany, circa 1950s; car 5 1/2" long, cycle 3 1/2" long. ($200-500) *Courtesy of Dunbar Moonlight Kid Auctions.*

Hubley die-cast cop cycle was a cheaper version of Hubley's cast-iron line and was only made for a short period of time. Circa late-1930s, with removable driver, 8" long. (Rare—$200-600) *Courtesy of Dunbar Moonlight Kid Auctions.*

1941 Harley-Davidson giveaway marble game. It has been rumored that these games have been reproduced. ($30-75) *Courtesy of Bob "Sprocket "Eckardt.*

185

Tin windup motorcycle with racing driver, Technofix, from West Germany. Circa 1950s, 7" long. ($100-300) *Courtesy of Dunbar Moonlight Kid Auctions.*

Hip Santa on motorcycle, bisque figure, circa 1920s, 2" long. ($30-75) *Courtesy of the Dunbar Moonlight Kid Collection.*

Pair of tin Japanese friction motorcycles, circa 1960, portraying a military policeman and a racer, both 3 1/2" long. ($10-40 each) *Courtesy of the Dunbar Moonlight Kid Collection* .

Technofix Zundapp Bella tin friction scooter, circa 1950s, from West Germany, 6 1/2" long. ($100-500) *Courtesy of Dunbar Moonlight Kid Auctions.*

Fantasy Items

The following Indian promotional items have popped up at various meets and shows. Their origin is dubious, since they never appeared in any Indian accessory catalogs, nor are they authenticated by any longtime collectors or Indian dealers. What's more, they have all turned up within the same time frame and in the same quantity. Because of the lack of any creditable verbal or published confirmation as to their authenticity, my opinion is that these are contemporary fantasy items and I have labeled them as such. They may have been portrayed as vintage since it is unclear who actually owns the Indian Motocycle Company trademark rights, so therefore any current manufacture would be in violation of trademark laws.

The marbles and rulers were sold to me by a dealer who, as of the writing of this book, was still selling the marbles. The shop rag, pocket mirror, and coin were consigned to one of our auctions as part of an Indian memorabilia collection and subsequently withdrawn from the sale. The dice were purchased from a longtime dealer who was as surprised as we were to find out that they were new. Anyone who has any further information regarding these pieces or others, please contact me at the address given in the back of the book. I did not give a price range as it's very difficult at this time to really ascertain market value for these items.

Also included is a reproduction Excelsior fob made about twenty years ago.

Indian silver half dollar commemorating company's 50th anniversary. *Courtesy of Dunbar Moonlight Kid Auctions.*

Indian cloth shop rag with solemn indian logo, 12" x 15". *Courtesy of Dunbar Moonlight Kid Auctions.*

Indian stainless steel ruler, 6". *Courtesy of Dunbar Moonlight Kid Auctions.*

Indian Motocycle pocket mirror, 2" x 3". *Courtesy of Dunbar Moonlight Kid Auctions.*

Package of six Indian 50th Anniversary souvenir marbles. *Courtesy of Dunbar Moonlight Kid Auctions.*

Pair of Indian Motocycles dice, 1/2" square. *Courtesy of Dunbar Moonlight Kid Auctions.*

Excelsior Auto Cycle brass fob, diecut with embossed motorcycle on face, "I am a loyal member of the Clan Excelsior—always on the job" on reverse, manufactured by Geo. Watch out for anything marked "Geo," it's a reproduction made about twenty years ago. 1 1/2" x 1 1/2". *Courtesy of Bob "Sprocket" Eckardt.*

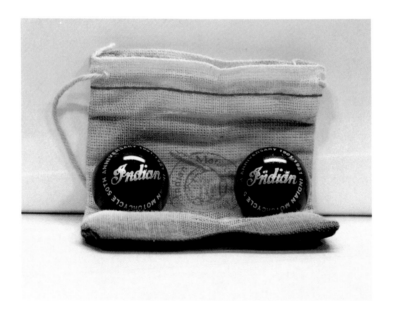

Indian 50th Anniversary souvenir marbles and cloth bag with solemn Indian logo. *Courtesy of Dunbar Moonlight Kid Auctions.*

Bibliography

Dunbar, Leila. *Motorcycle Collectibles with Values.* (Atglen, Pa.: Schiffer Publishing, 1996)

Ferrar, Ann. *Hear Me Roar.* (New York: Crown Publishers, 1996)

Girdler, Allan. *Harley-Davidson, The American Motorcycle.* (Osceola, Wis.: Motorbooks International, 1992)

Hatfield, Jerry. *Indian Motorcycle Photographic History.* (Osceola, Wis.: Motorbooks International, 1993)

Hatfield, Jerry. *American Racing Motorcycles.* (Osceola, Wis.: Motorbooks International, 1989)

Hatfield, Jerry & Hans Halberstadt. *Indian Motorcycles.* (Osceola, Wis.: Motorbooks International, 1996)

Kanter, Buzz. *Indian Motorcycles.* (Osceola, Wis.: Motorbooks International, 1993

Karolevitz, Bob. *Yesterday's Motorcycles.* Mission Hill, S.D.: Dakota Homestead Publishers, 1986)

Mitchel, Doug. *The Harley-Davidson Chronicle.* (Lincolnwood, Ill.: Publications International, Ltd., 1996)

Prior, Rupert. *Motorcycling: The Golden Years.* (London: Tiger Books International, PLC, 1994)

Rae, Ronald L. *The Goulding Album.* (Ronald L. Rae, 1996)

Sucher, Harry V. *American Motorcycling.* (Laguna Niguel, Calif.: Infosport, July 1995)

Wagner, Herbert. *Harley-Davidson, 1930-41.* (Atglen, Pa.: Schiffer Publishing, 1996)

Wilson, Hugo. *The Ultimate Motorcycle Book.* (New York: Dorling Kindersley, 1993)

Wright, David K. *The Harley-Davidson Motor Company, An Official Ninety-Year History.* Third Edition. (Osceola, Wis.: Motorbooks International, 1993)

Wright, Stephen. *American Racer, 1900-1939.* (Osceola, Wis.: Motorbooks International, 1979)

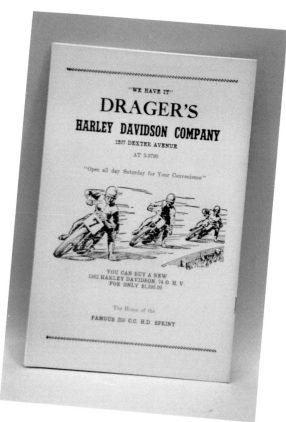